# HOW TO DRAW 'PLANES

By

FRANK A. A. WOOTTON

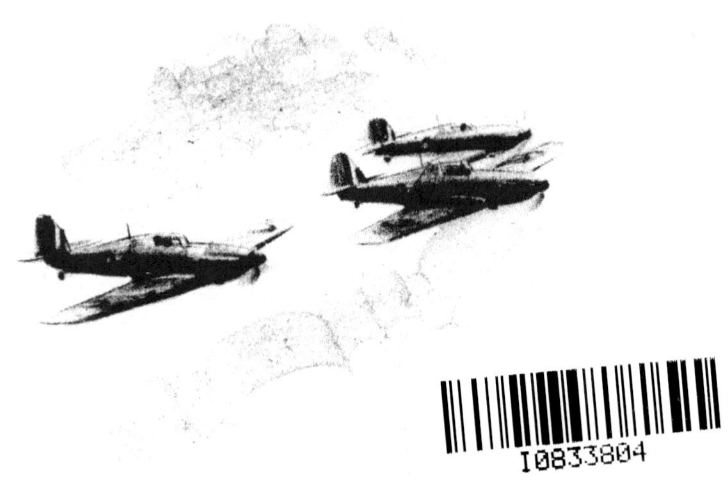


COACHWHIP PUBLICATIONS
Greenville, Ohio

*How to Draw Planes*, by Frank A. A. Wootton

First published 1941.
Front cover: The "Bottisham Four" P-51 Mustangs, USAAF

ISBN 1-61646-206-X
ISBN-13 978-1-61646-206-2

CoachwhipBooks.com

# CONTENTS



Aircraft illustrated include the "Airacobra"; "Albacore"; "Anson"; "Beaufighter"; "Blenheim"; "Beaufort"; "Boston"; "Catalina"; "Defiant"; "Fortress"; "Fulmar"; "Gladiator"; "Halifax"; "Hampden"; "Hurricane"; "Lysander"; "Manchester"; "Oxford"; "Roc"; "Spitfire"; "Stirling"; "Sunderland"; "Tomahawk"; and the "Wellington."

## ACKNOWLEDGMENTS

Thanks are due to Mr. Loader of Samson Clark & Co. Ltd., and The de Havilland Aircraft Co. Ltd., for their help and permission to reproduce paintings on pages 45, 47 and 48. Thanks are also due to Dowty Equipment Ltd., for the painting reproduced on page 51, and to A. V. Roe & Co. Ltd., and Armstrong Siddeley Motors Ltd., for the painting reproduced on page 61.

# INTRODUCTION

Aircraft today are very much in the front line and I think that a good many of you will be familiar with the best known types. To be able to distinguish between these types is to appreciate the design of them and in some cases to recognise the subtle differences between one design and another.

Early designers of aircraft used to model their designs on the shape of birds. At that period they lacked the knowledge of construction that designers have today, so that their efforts were not so clean and streamlined as 'planes are now.

It was not until designers could make their 'planes stay up with some margin of safety that design was considered or was given any research. Then, research took them back to the bird which they knew to be aerodynamically perfect ; afterwards, however they studied form and not merely shape. Since that time aircraft have lost their angles and multitudinous spars, engines are now built in and wheels disappear ; birdlike forms have evolved. Clearness of function has produced aircraft that are beautiful to look at and safe to fly.

People sometimes ask me why I paint aircraft. I can never give them a satisfactory answer as I know they would not ask the question if they could appreciate aircraft as I do. We are slow to acknowledge beauty in mechanics ; the locomotive is almost dead before it has become easy to look at, though it has lived a hundred years. The 'plane in its early forties has caught us up and is rapidly leaving some of us behind, slow to appreciate.

My aim in this book is to try and put before you the aircraft of today, to show you how to appreciate their inherent design, and how to express what you see and feel about them.

FRANK A. A. WOOTTON.

# PREFACE TO REVISED EDITION

There are marked changes in the later designs of aircraft due to new conceptions of their purpose in air warfare. Various factors such as speed, vision and loads have necessitated considerable variations in their appearance.

You will see these changes in the new illustrations with which this revised edition of " How to Draw 'Planes " has been brought up to date.

While including the latest types of which details can be published, I have retained most of their forerunners so that the new developments can be compared.

F.A.A.W.

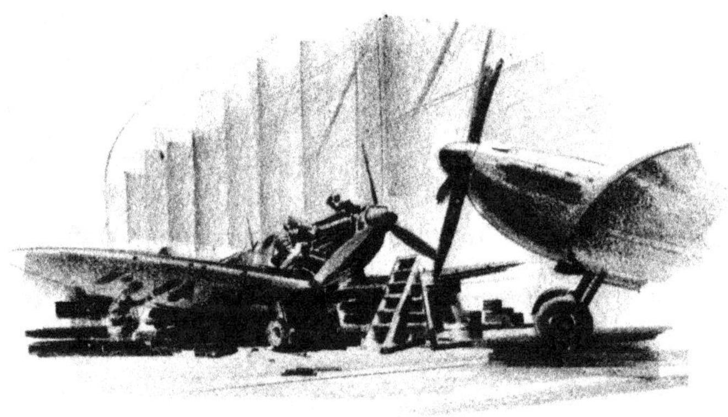

# CONSTRUCTION

If you could see a 'plane in the course of construction, without its outer covering of metal and fabric, you would see a mass of skeleton-like ribs, sections and longerons.

Even at this stage, those of you who can recognise the types of 'planes by their characteristic shape, would no doubt be able to tell what 'plane was under construction.

A preliminary framework is essential for everything you draw, so you will find that careful work when laying out your drawing in its first stages will go farther than anything else towards making a good drawing.

It will not be necessary of course for you to construct your drawing with so much framework as that used in building aircraft but some construction is necessary to make your drawing look right. Without this building up, your pencil would tend to run away from you, with the result that your drawing would be weak and open to criticism.

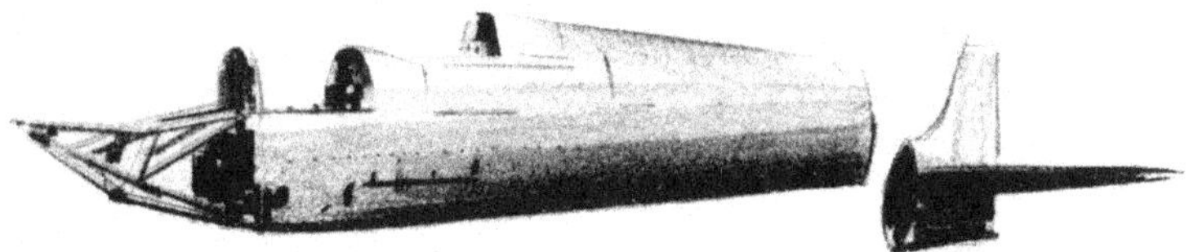

*Fuselage and Fin of 'Spitfire.'*

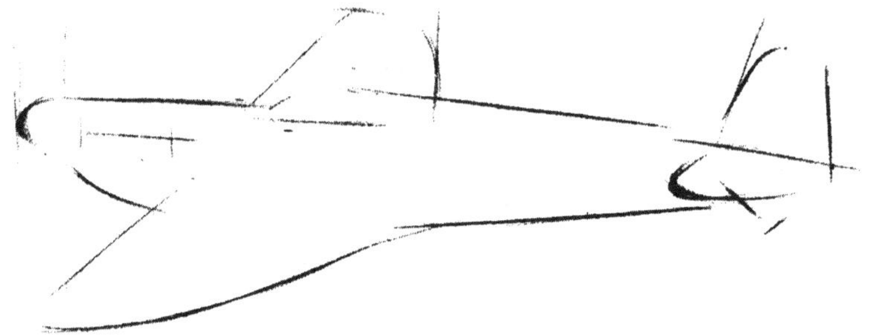

Everything depends on these lines; they decide the angle of viewpoint and length and breadth of the drawing. The proportions of every part of the 'plane are controlled by these first construction lines.

Make sure your perspective is correct on the main lines of the wings and tail, study the angles that the wing and tail make through the fuselage or body of the 'plane.

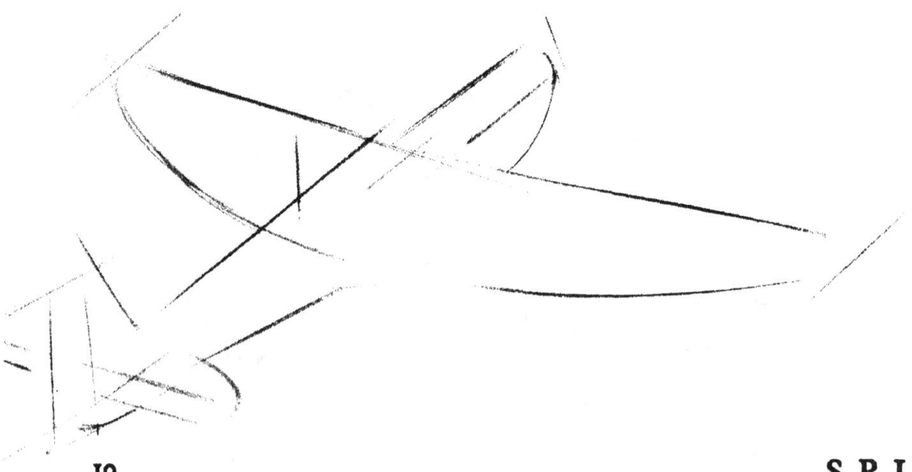

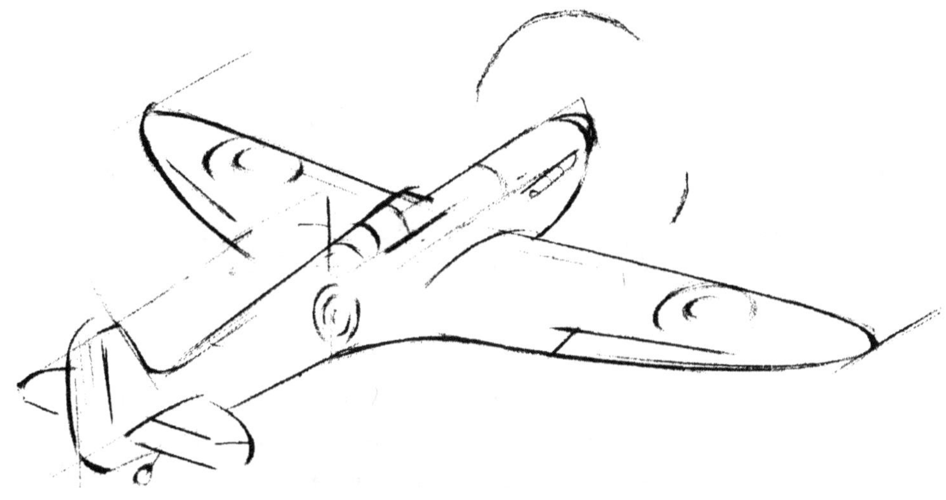

Draw these first lines lightly with a pencil, so lightly that they are only just there, don't rub out every wrong line as you do it, correct the faulty lines and save the cleaning up process until you are sure that you have got the right lines.

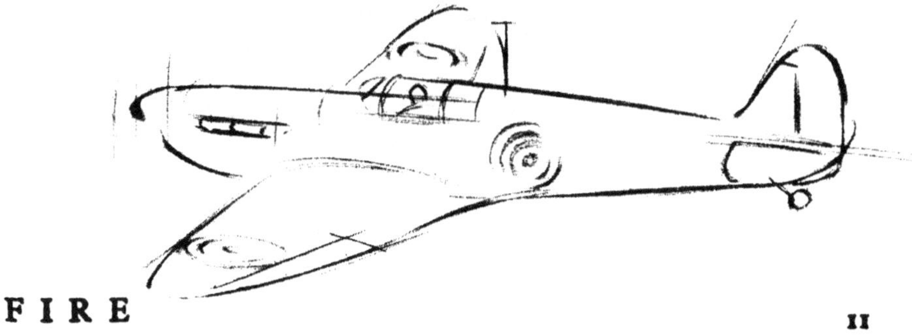

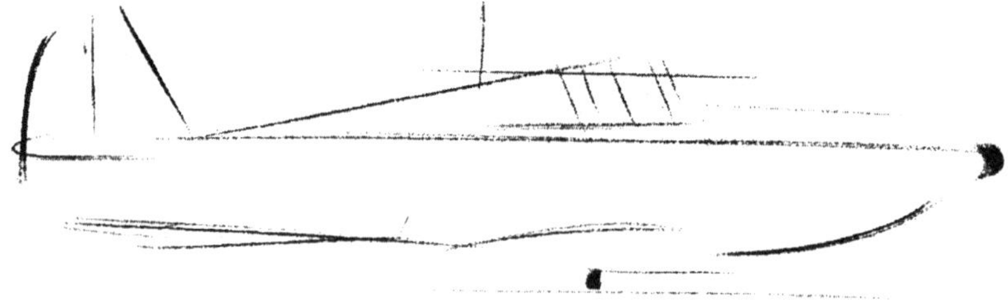

When you draw these first lines, do not worry too much about the shape or form of each individual part of the 'plane, look at the 'plane as a whole and concentrate on the main lines.

For these drawings I have chosen the ' Spitfire ' and the ' Hurricane.' You will have noticed in the lines of the ' Spitfire ' the straight line along the top of the fuselage, unbroken from tail to nose except where it steps down the windscreen to continue along

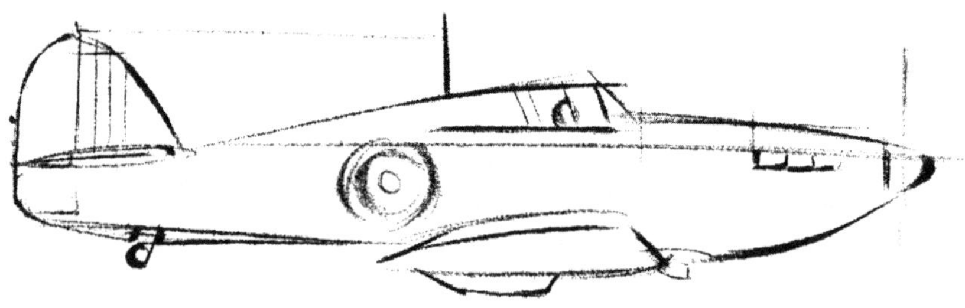



HURRI

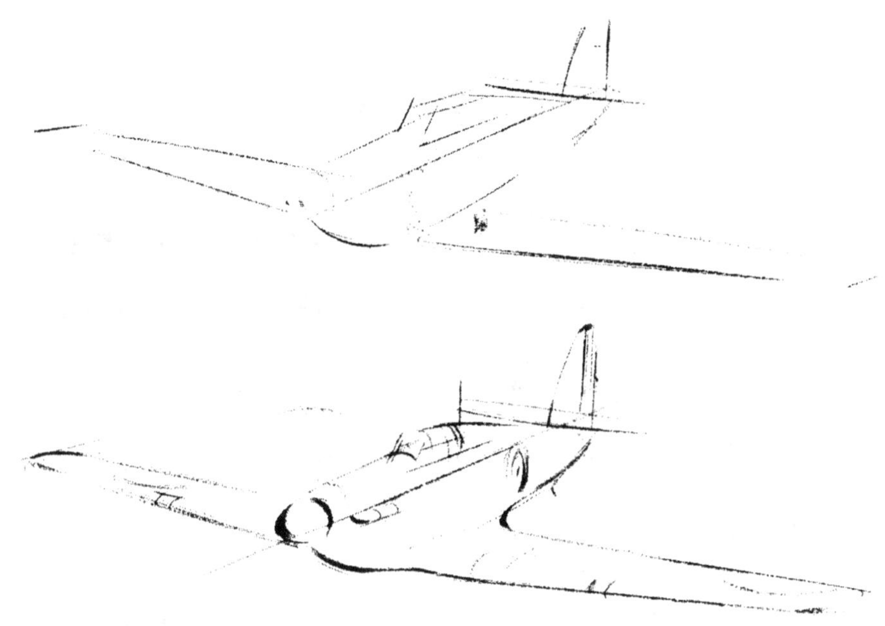

the engine cowling. These straight lines are most useful when laying out the drawing. The 'Hurricane' has few straight lines in the fuselage so that when drawing this machine, draw an imaginary line from the centre of the propeller boss, along the top of the exhaust pipes and finishing where the tail joins the fuselage. This line combined with the straight edges of the wings will help you in drawing this machine.

CANE

# CONSTRUCTION

The next step is accurately to draw in the curves of the wings, tail and fin. The lines of the fuselage should also be given special attention. Extra care should be taken over these as sometimes they make all the difference between two similar 'planes such as the ' Spitfire ' and the ' Hurricane.'

Draw in the transparent hood which covers the pilot's cockpit; this slides back on the actual machine on an external channel piece which runs parallel to the lines I have mentioned on the fuselage of both machines. Do not make too much of the framework of the transparent parts; the frame is as thin as the designers can make it. A thick frame would obstruct the pilot's vision.

## c o n t i n u e d

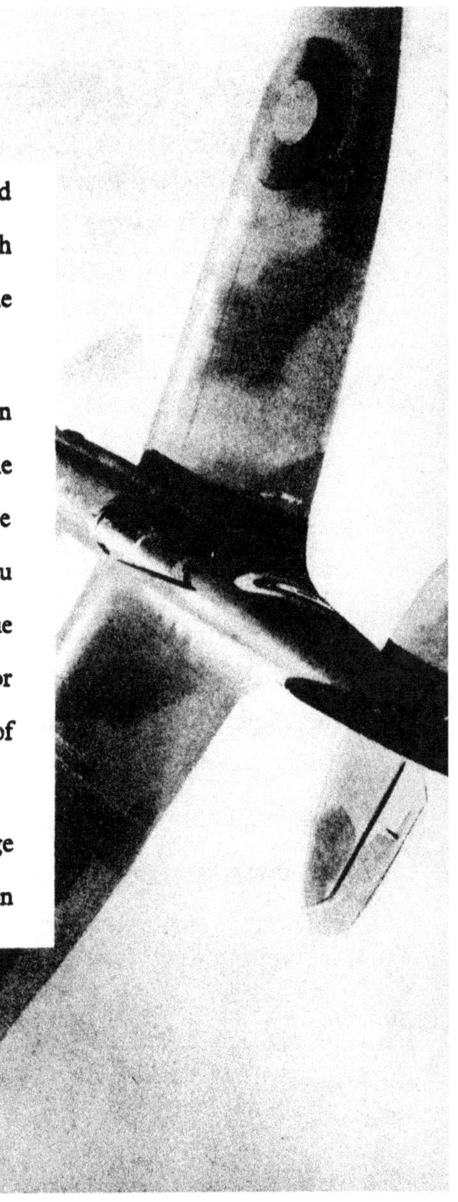

The external exhaust pipes are placed well forward and high in the nose of both fighters as they are now fitted with the same type of engine.

One or two special points to watch when finishing the drawing. Wherever possible try to show the form or shape of the section of that part of the machine you are drawing. The red, white and blue roundels painted on R.A.F. machines for instance. Make them take the shape of the section on which they are painted.

The cockpit cover cutting into the fuselage viewed from an angle will give the section of the top part of the fuselage.

# DRAWING A BOMBER

The two fighter 'planes were not difficult as they presented no real problems in drawing. However you will find that when you attempt a drawing of a radial engined 'plane there are real problems unless you know the rule that governs elipses.

For the present, here are the first lines of a bomber 'plane, the Bristol ' Blenheim.' The procedure for laying out this 'plane is of course exactly the same as I have shown you for the fighters.

The position of the 'plane and then the proportions are lightly mapped out.

In my first rough layout you will see the engines are very vaguely indicated and are considered simply as cylindrical shapes. Later they begin to take the shape of the actual engine but they are not finally drawn in until the elipses are correctly drawn.

You will notice that the engines of the 'plane are not the only round shapes ; the gun turret at this stage of the drawing is also regarded as a cylinder and similarly the half round shape of the forward part of the fuselage is treated as a complete cylinder.

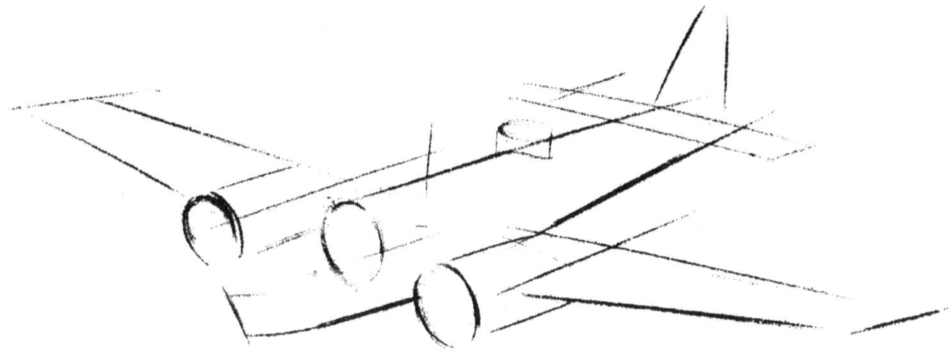

These elipses are drawn at an angle to conform with the general perspective of the drawing, and it is this angle which is so important. This angle is governed by a simple rule which I will explain to you.

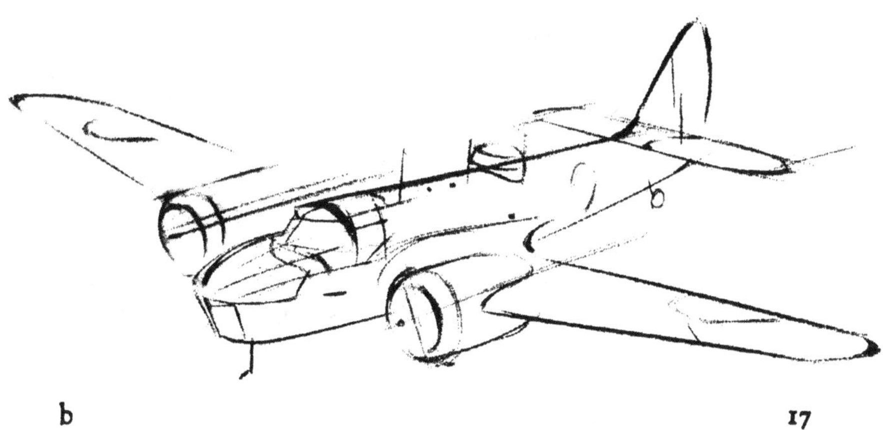

# ELIPSES

'Planes when you draw them have their share of elipses, in the form of radial engines, wheels, etc., so if you have any difficulty in drawing these elipses, here is the easiest method for you to draw them. Remember the method, as most mechanical things you draw will have an elipse.

A properly constructed elipse must have an Axis and an Axle. These are straight lines at right angles to each other. Draw them with a ruler like this and be certain that they are exactly at right angles. Decide for yourself the proportions the elipse is to take and mark off the length and breadth, then to help me explain the method, mark

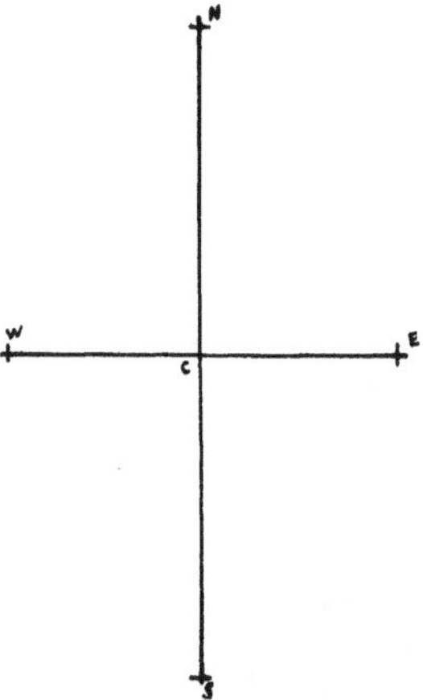


this practice one with North, South, East and West with a C for the centre. The longer line of the two is the Axis and the short line is the Axle no matter which way up the elipse is to be.

## a n d

Now, a line from North has got to describe a nice curve until it meets West to make a perfect quarter of the elipse. You will need a strip of paper with a straight edge. Place the straight edge against the Axis and mark off exactly N and C, turn the strip horizontally and place it against the Axle with the N mark exactly on W, now mark off C again which will come somewhere between N and the first C previously marked. Now place your strip upright again, as you were, with N on N and lower C on C. Move the strip slowly keeping middle C moving down the line N to S, and C moving along West to East. If you do this carefully and at the same time watch what N is doing, you will see that it follows a very nice curve that you will want to put on paper. To do this, move the paper in easy stages marking the position of N at intervals. Join up these marks with a good freehand curve and trace it off on to the other three quarters of the elipse.

A mechanical method it is true but then you are drawing a mechanical shape. When you have drawn several this way you will find that you will be able to draw them freehand more easily than you could before.

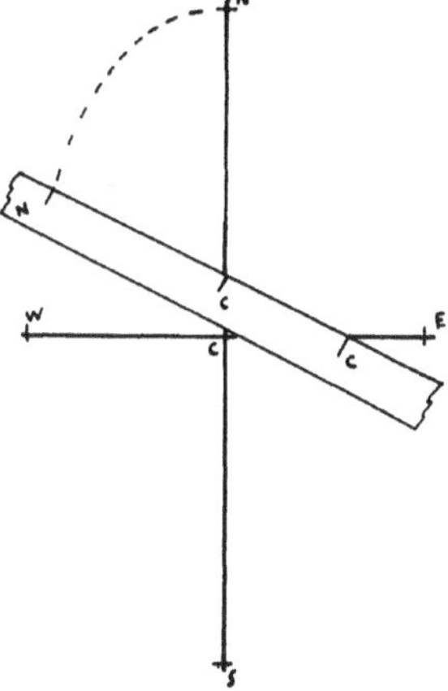

# how to apply them

Now that you have your elipse made easy for you, there is only one way of applying it to your drawing.

Please remember this important rule for all elipses.

The Axis is always at right angles to the Axle. At first this will not convey much to you, but every elipse you draw whether it is for a radial engine or the rim of a teacup, imagine that it is a wheel with an axle passing through its centre.

Your elipse the way I have explained it already has a very good Axis and Axle, and no matter what the perspective or angle of your elipse these two always remain at right angles to each other.

Here are some examples to prove the rule.

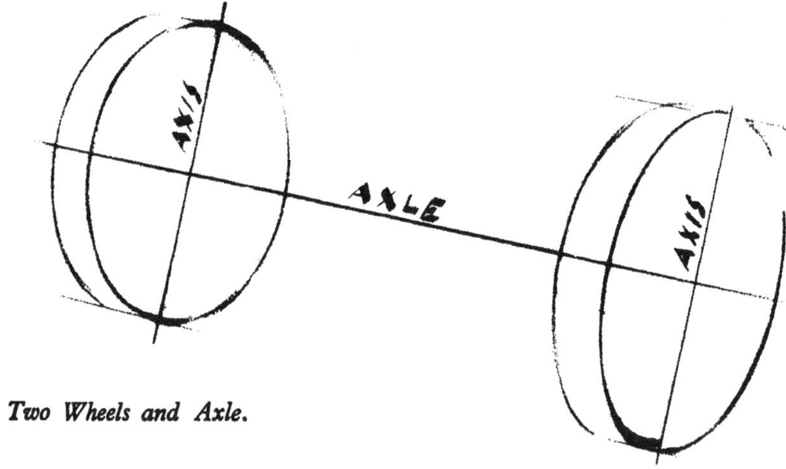


*Two Wheels and Axle.*

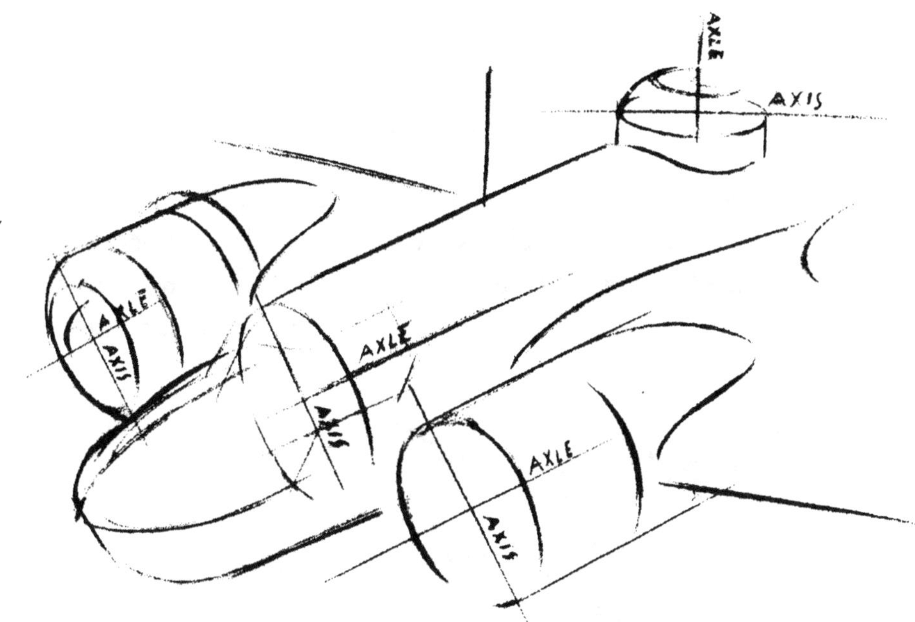


*Engine installation on a 'Blenheim'
Note – gun turret and pilots cockpit,*

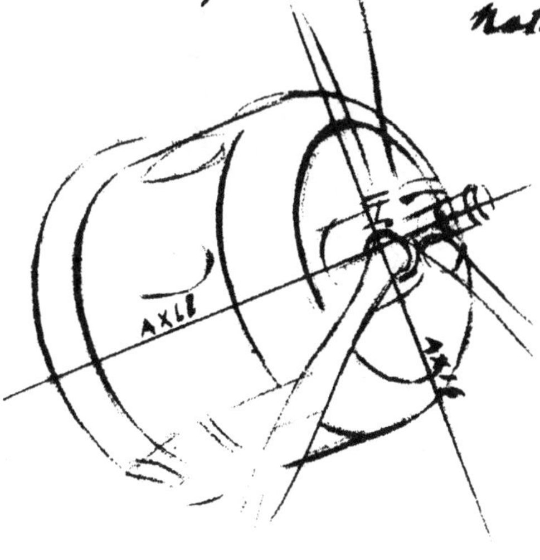

# DETAIL STUDIES

Although aircraft vary to conform with their duties, some components are similar in many respects. Radial engines for instance, power operated turrets and airscrews. These are made by specialist constructors and facilitate the work of the aircraft manufacturer.

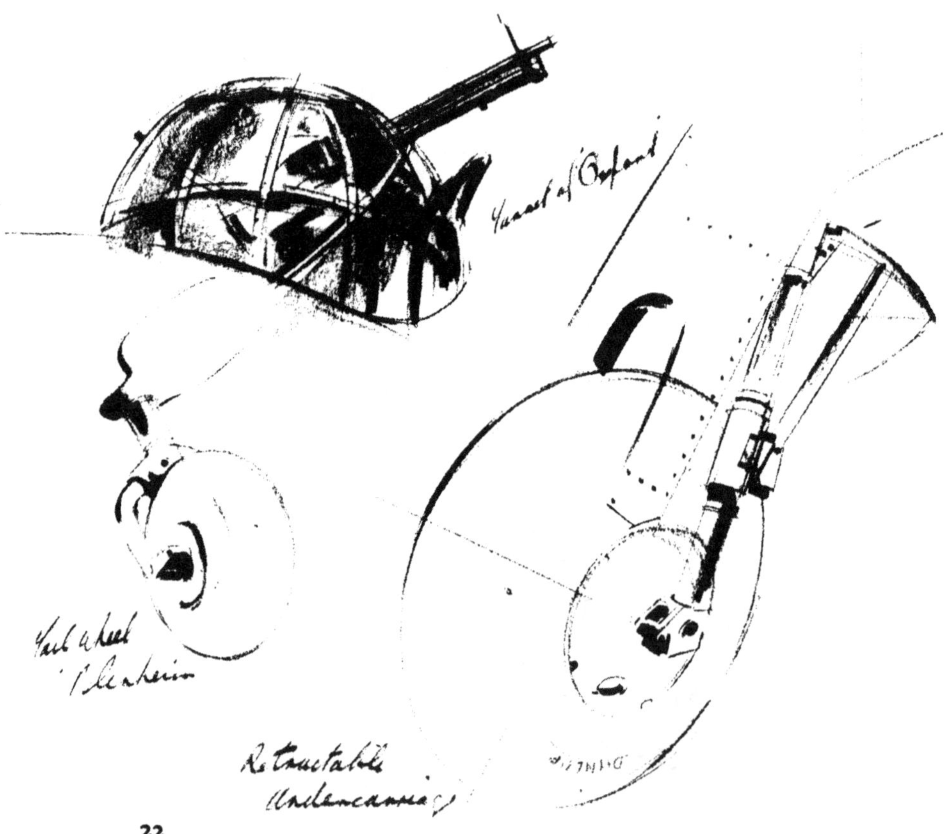

# OF COMPONENTS

You should take every advantage of this and make special studies of these components so that you will be familiar with them when it comes to applying them to your drawings.

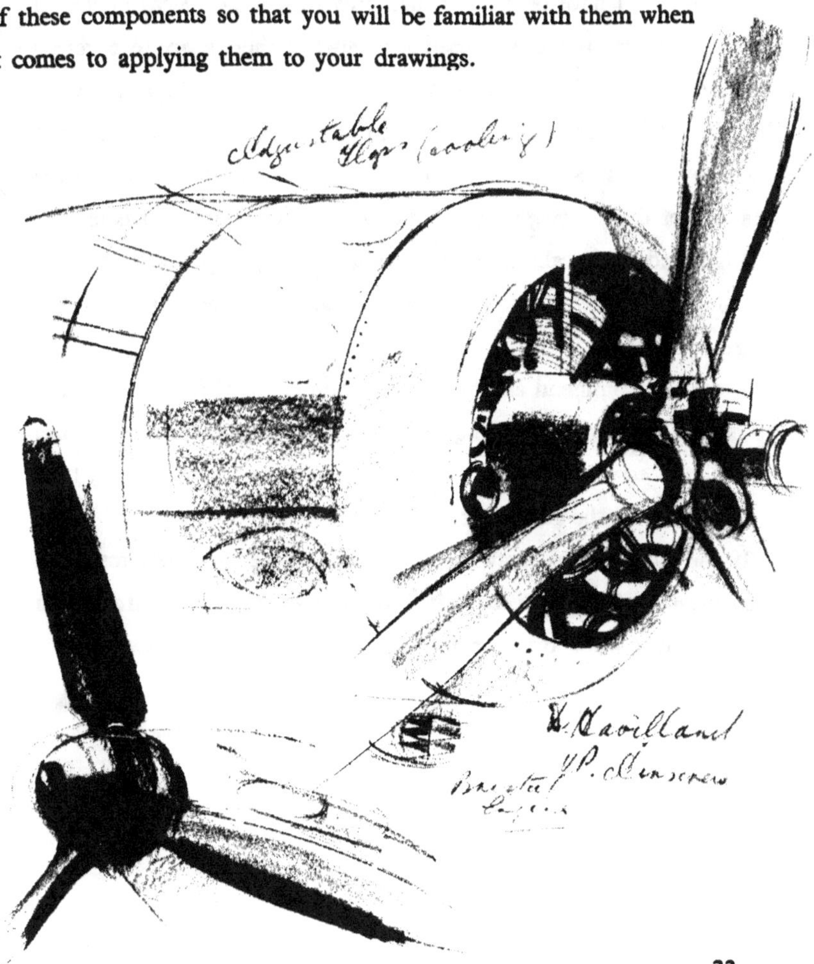

*Rotol airscrew.*

# LIGHT AND SHADE

Up to now I have been concerned only with the correct drawing of aircraft. It has not been possible in such a short space to cover all types of aircraft, in fact it was hardly necessary as all aircraft are based on the same principles of flight, and although they each have their characteristics I hope to cover some of these while bringing the drawing of them a stage further into a study of light and shade.

Light and shade calls for a careful study as it will give form to your drawing and will help some of you to get over the pencil outline stage.

I cannot recommend anything better than charcoal for the medium. It has the advantages of being easily applied, a good range of tones and is very easy to rub out. If charcoal is out of the question, then a soft pencil is the next best thing.

If you wish to keep drawings made with these two mediums, then they must be fixed. Fixative is expensive to buy so I will tell you how to make your own fixative which will be inexpensive.

Formula for making fixative. To 1 part white shellac, 1 part turpentine, 9 parts methylated spirit. Mix well. This will protect your drawing as though it were varnish and should be sprayed on the drawing with a vaporizer.

With charcoal you will find putty rubber or kneaded rubber useful for picking out highlights. For smoothing charcoal once it is applied a paper stump or Tortillon is not so smeary as fingers. A stump is made from special soft blotting-like paper rolled in the form of a big pencil.

I make all my rough drawings with charcoal on detail paper which I buy in the form of a large pad.

Charcoal should be a good black and must be soft for smooth application.

In making these tone studies of aircraft the point of the charcoal was not used except for thin outlines.

# LIGHT AND SHADE

To return to aircraft again, for these light and shade studies I have chosen 'planes that are widely different as regards actual form. The view points were also considered with an eye to the characteristics of the aircraft.

Some I have drawn against the light, as this form of lighting gives an opportunity to show the silhouette to advantage. Cast shadows are sometimes useful, for instance in the first drawing of the 'Spitfire' the fuselage casts a shadow on to the wing, the cast shadow helping to show the curved surface of the wing.

Remember that cast shadow is always darker than shade, except perhaps when it is thrown on to a transparent surface.

The second drawing of the 'Spitfire' is a study of the 'plane with the light coming from above, a more universal light which finds the top surfaces of the 'planes and runs along the upper surfaces of the fuselage. Although it is not such an exciting light as the first, it does give a true idea of the form of the 'plane.

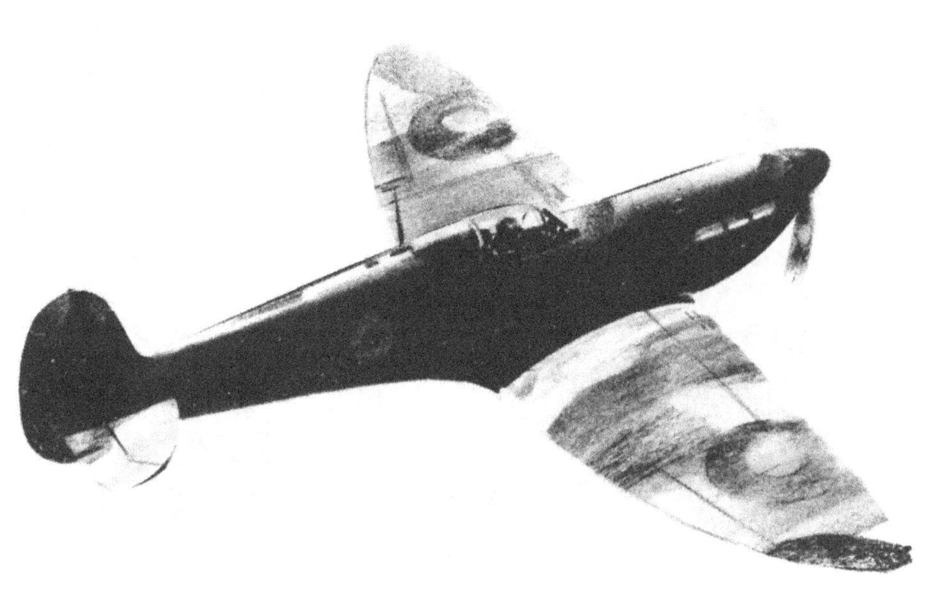

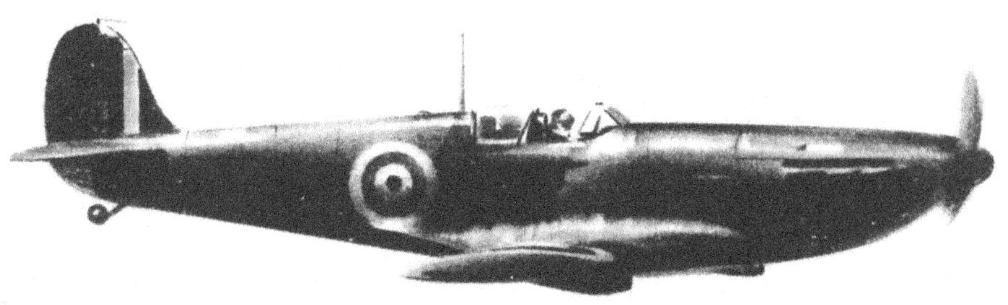

SPITFIRE

L I G H T   A N D

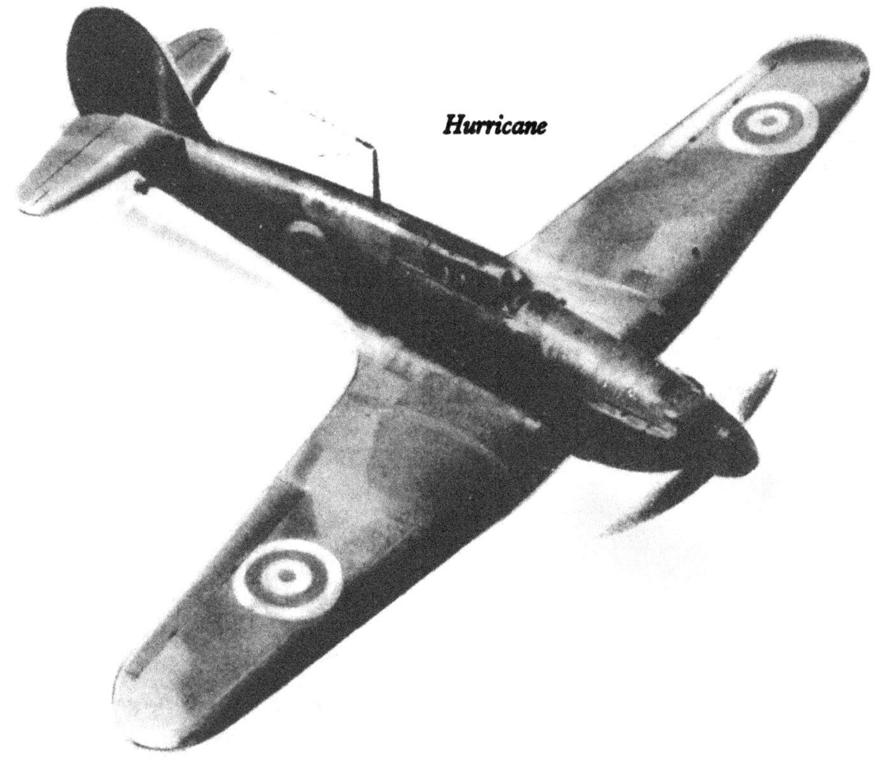
*Hurricane*

*Charcoal Studies.*

# S H A D E

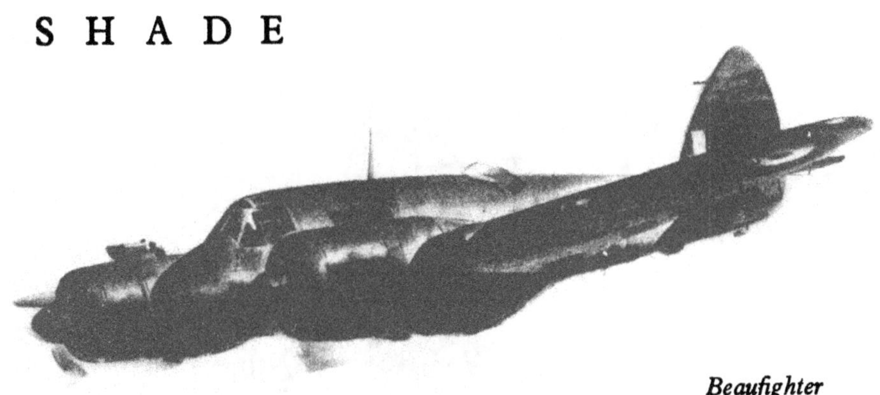

*Beaufighter*

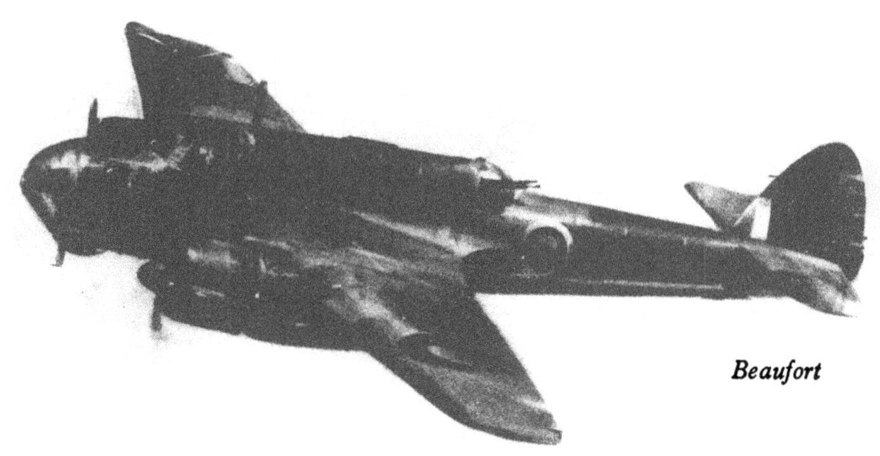

*Beaufort*

# L I G H T   A N D

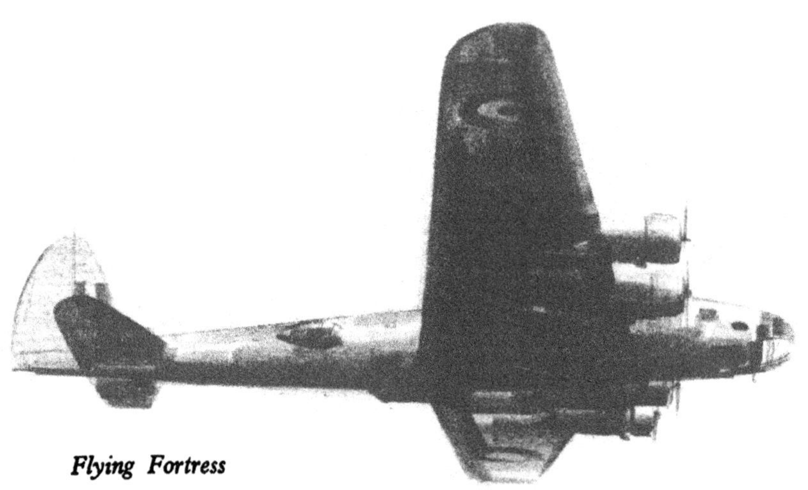

*Flying Fortress*

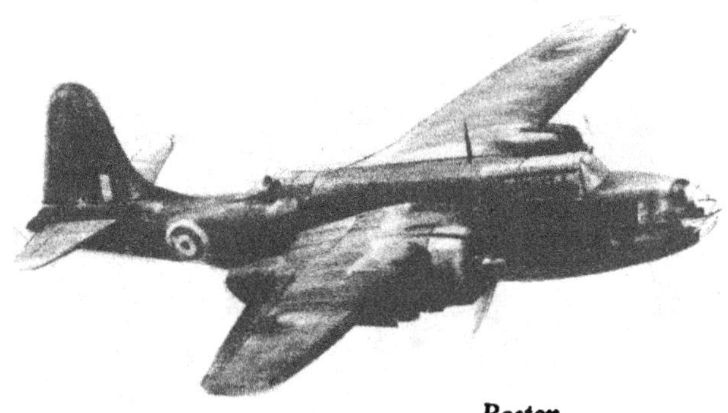

*Boston*

# S H A D E

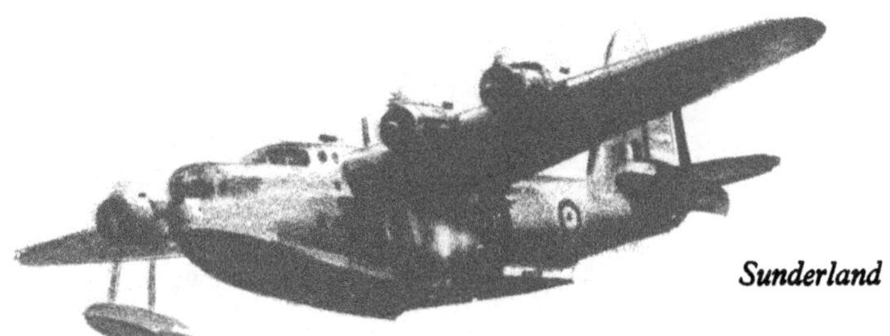

*Sunderland*

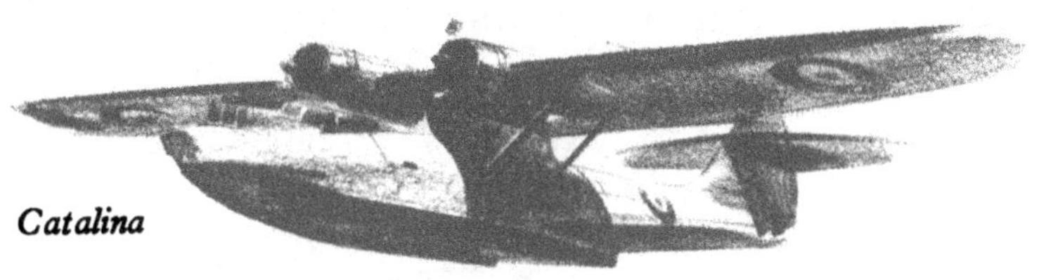

*Catalina*

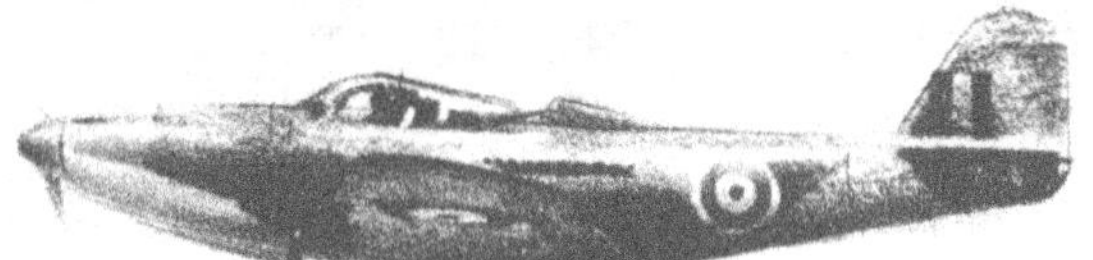

*Airacobra*

# LIGHT AND SHADE

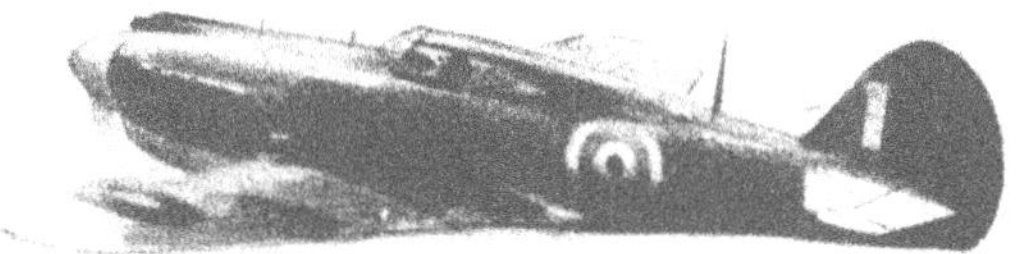

*Tomahawk*

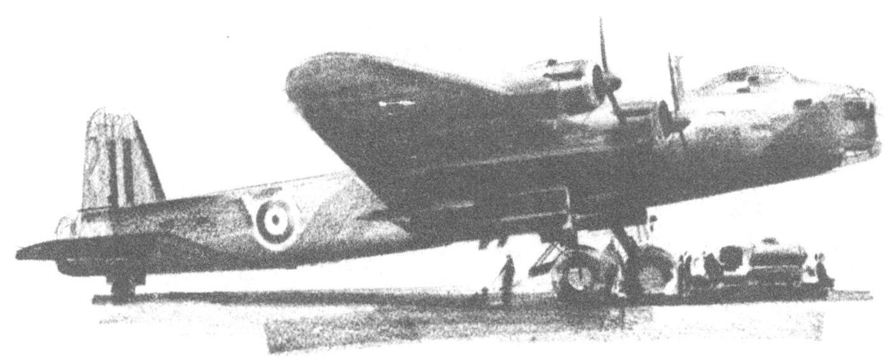

*Stirling*

I cannot think of any better way to show the impressive size of the 'Stirling' than to draw it on the ground where it appears to dwarf the airmen working on the machine.

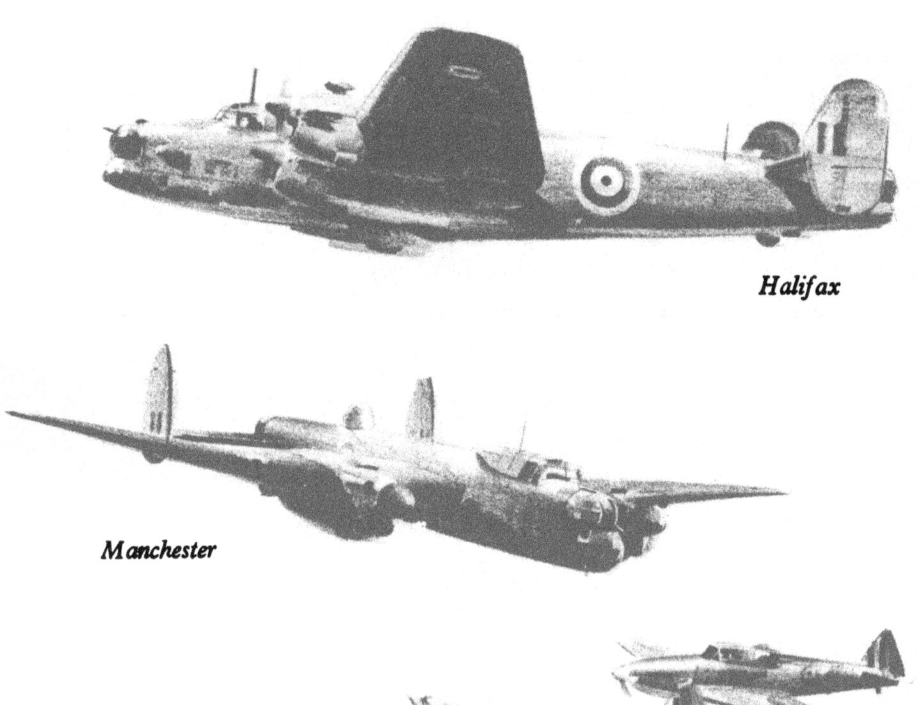

*Halifax*

*Manchester*

*Defiants*

If you find it difficult to put on a flat tone with a pencil, try extracting a small piece of lead and using it flat as you would charcoal.

# LIGHT AND SHADE

Treat all transparent surfaces lightly, as on these highly reflective surfaces the lights will be brighter and the darks lighter. Do not let the colour of any particular part of the 'plane deceive you as regards its true tone value. Black painted surfaces can in certain circumstances reflect a high light that even pure white paper could not give you, so it is natural that in between such a contrast from the actual colour you will find many middle tones. Similarly, white painted surfaces sometimes have highlights themselves and since your brightest white is your white paper, you must not allow yourself to be trapped into thinking that parts of the aircraft painted white must necessarily be white on your drawing. Try to get variety into your drawings by making the most of lighting and its effects.

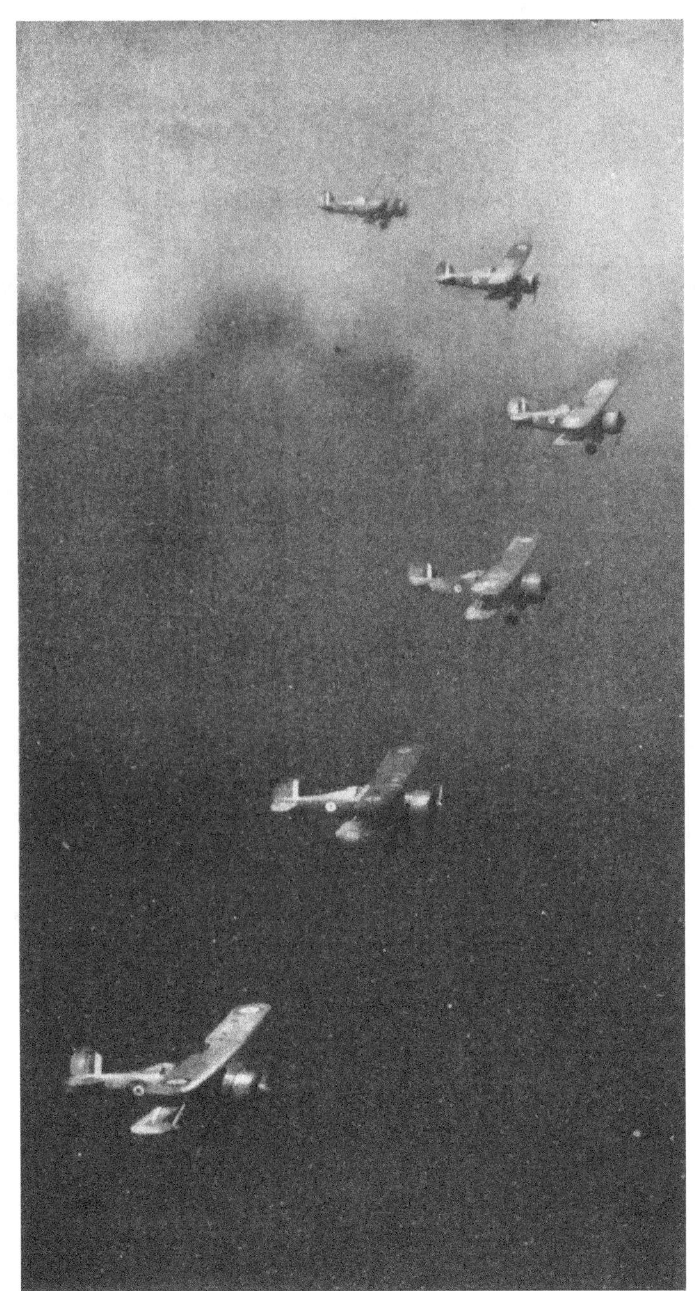

*Gloster 'Gladiators.'*

# LIGHT AND SHADE

When painting camouflaged aircraft, do not make the pattern too contrasty in tone if you wish to preserve the lines of the 'plane. I know that the object of camoudlage is to break up the general outline, but then your job is to illustrate the 'plane and not to hide it. The camouflage problem can be overcome by lighting; parts of the 'plane can be thrown in shadow and other parts in brilliant light. This effectively breaks up the effect of camouflage.

# COMPOSITION

When you can draw 'planes satisfactorily you will want to put them into a picture and I daresay that a good many of you will have had some experience of composing a picture dealing with aircraft. In composing a picture, have you ever felt that your drawing had perhaps too much space with nothing of interest in it, or on the other hand felt that some part was rather too crowded? Sometimes too when you show your drawing to somebody else, they look at the wrong part first or they do not seem to see exactly what the picture is meant to illustrate. Well, that is where a knowledge of composition will lend you a hand and help you to get over some of the difficulties that crop up when making a picture.

Composition is a very wide subject. I cannot hope to cover it in these few pages so I will try instead to show you how composition affects a picture.

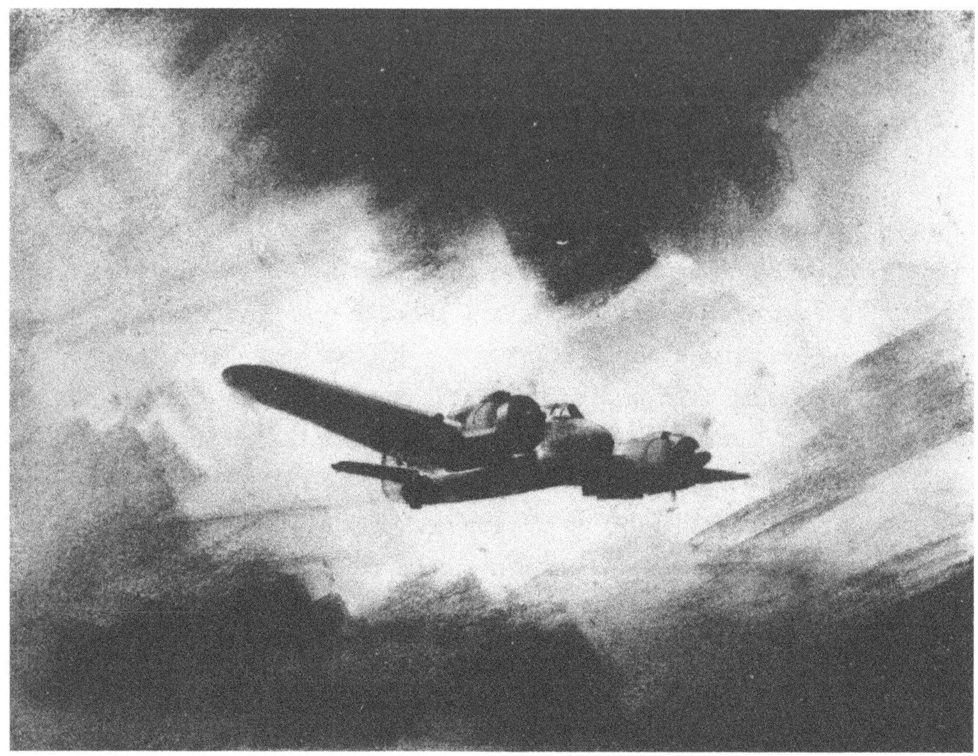

In this picture of a ' Beaufighter ' I want you to notice the white clouds behind the 'plane and the way they form a V shape or a rough arrow head. At the point of the V is the 'plane.

It is natural that your eye should run to the point of two converging lines such as these. The 'plane was placed where it is so that when you first look at the picture, your eye is taken to the 'plane immediately. Notice too that it is silhouetted against the lightest and most unbroken part of the sky so that you find it easy to look at.

You might say that you cannot help but see the 'plane as it is the only one in the picture and doubt whether the cloud formation has the effect that I have pointed out. So to prove the usefulness of my clouds, I have altered the same picture to show how bad composition can confuse rather than help. Here I have upset the composition——

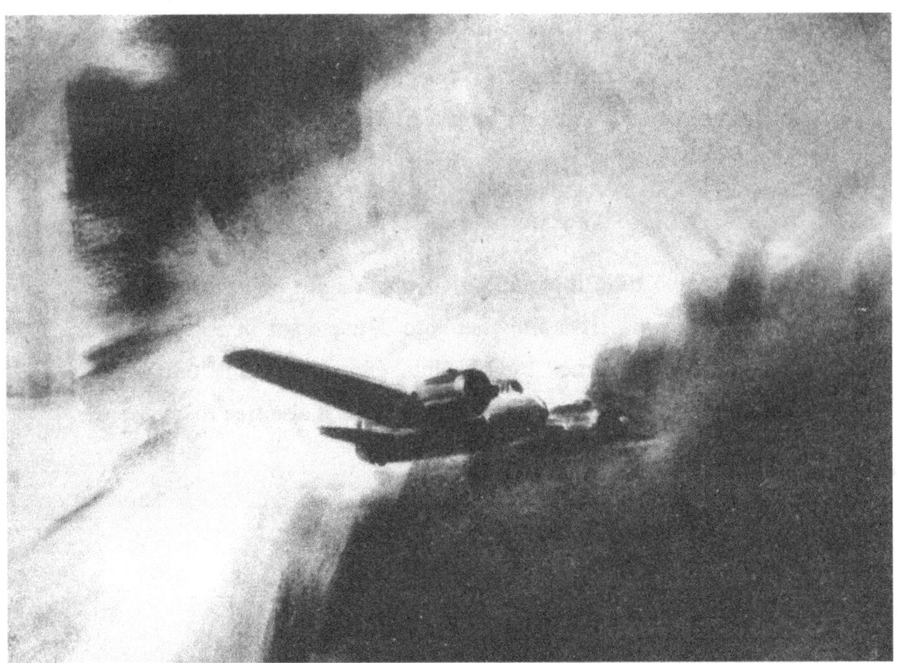

——Now it appears to be sitting on the edge of a cloud which tends to freeze any movement the 'plane might have and holds it immovable.

The V shape directional lines of the white clouds lead away from the 'plane taking the useful white background with it. Your eye still travels to the point of the V and although your eye returns to the 'plane there is the uncomfortable feeling that it is struggling against the whole pattern of things.

So you see how the composition, or arrangement if you like, affects a picture. The illustration I have given you was the most simple I could think of, the fewest of clouds and only one 'plane, a combination that calls for the minimum of design. More 'planes and a more complicated cloud formation would however need far more careful thought in designing the composition.

* * * *

There are no rules in composition that cannot be broken so I will not lay any down. It is impossible to define a list of rules, for it is an arrangement governed by individual expression. The units of the composition are the choice of the artist. He is also free to choose the number of units he employs, so that it remains for him to put them together in the best way possible.

For a beginning I can only advise you to watch the balance of tones and masses, to see that directional lines are controlled and used to help the composition and for the time being, keep your compositions simple, cut out all unnecessary planes and clouds and concentrate on making the most of very little.

Before attempting a finished picture, make one or two rough sketches of what you intend to do. These sketches can be quite small, not too small of course, but sufficient to give you a clear idea of the finished composition.

You will find that charcoal will be useful for making these roughs. Overleaf are three rough compositions which will give you some idea of the amount of drawing necessary.

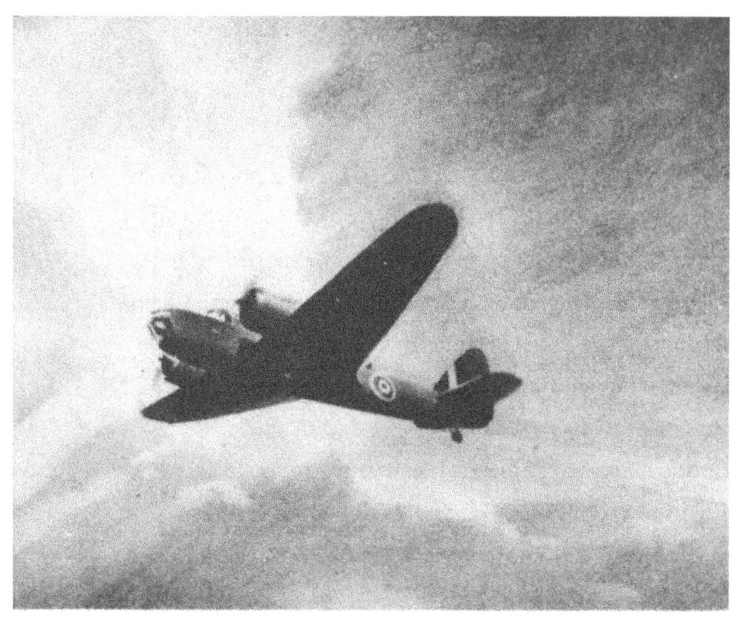

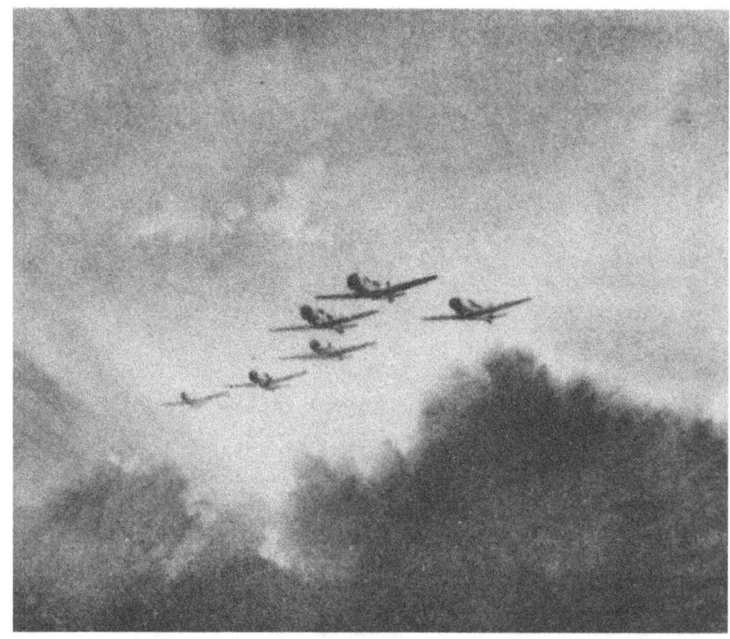

1. *Bristol 'Blenheim'*
2. *Blackburn 'Rocs'*
3. *Fairey 'Albacore'*

All three of these roughs are based on the same principle as the composition showing the 'Beaufighter.'

The directional lines in each illustration are made up of cloud formations, although I would like to point out that in the lower compositions the 'planes themselves, in their formations, play an important part in their relation to the composition.

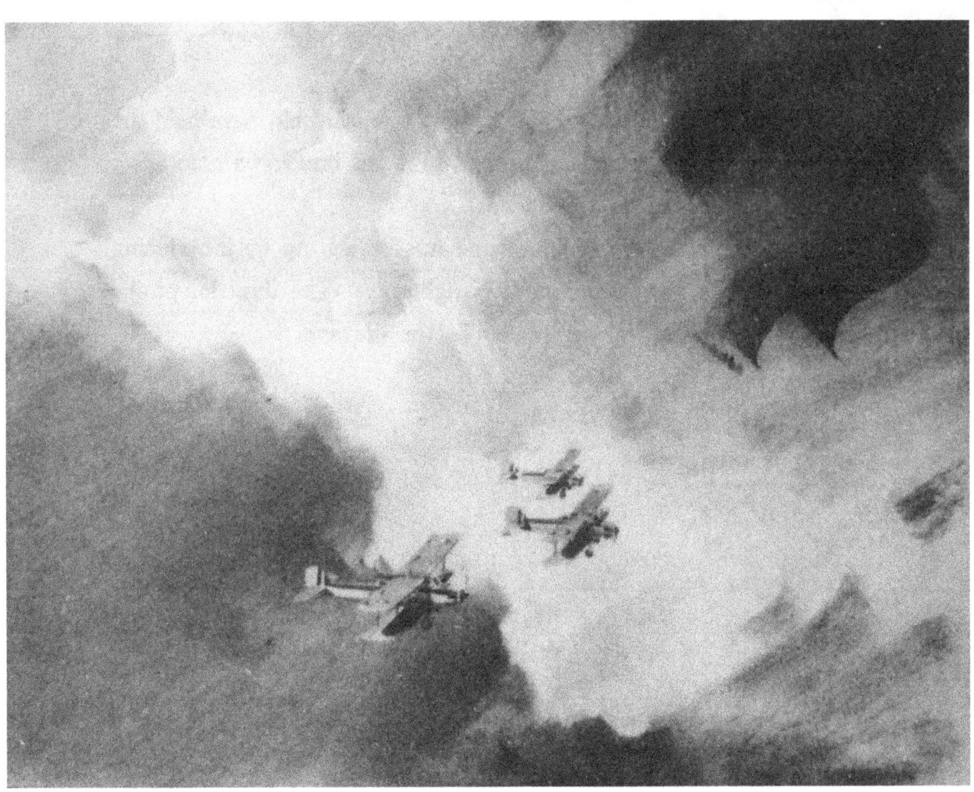

# COMPOSITION

This composition is rather different from those preceding, it is based on an entirely different principle. I have used radiation as the main theme.

The 'Wellingtons' are placed against the spreading light of dawn from which the clouds radiate.

One looks at the centre of the composition first as it contains the brightest light and the darkest tones. From this centre, rise the 'planes and the clouds, taking your eye with them in an upward direction. This incidentally helps to put over the fact that the 'planes are rising in a take-off and not landing.

The line of the horizon was not wanted as it would have held the eye too long in a horizontal direction, so it was broken with an effect as of a heavy localized ground mist.

The heavy mass of the foreground was broken up by introducing a patch of rain water reflecting the bright sky. The direction of the gully helps the general perspective of the drawing.

Wellingtons taking off at Dawn

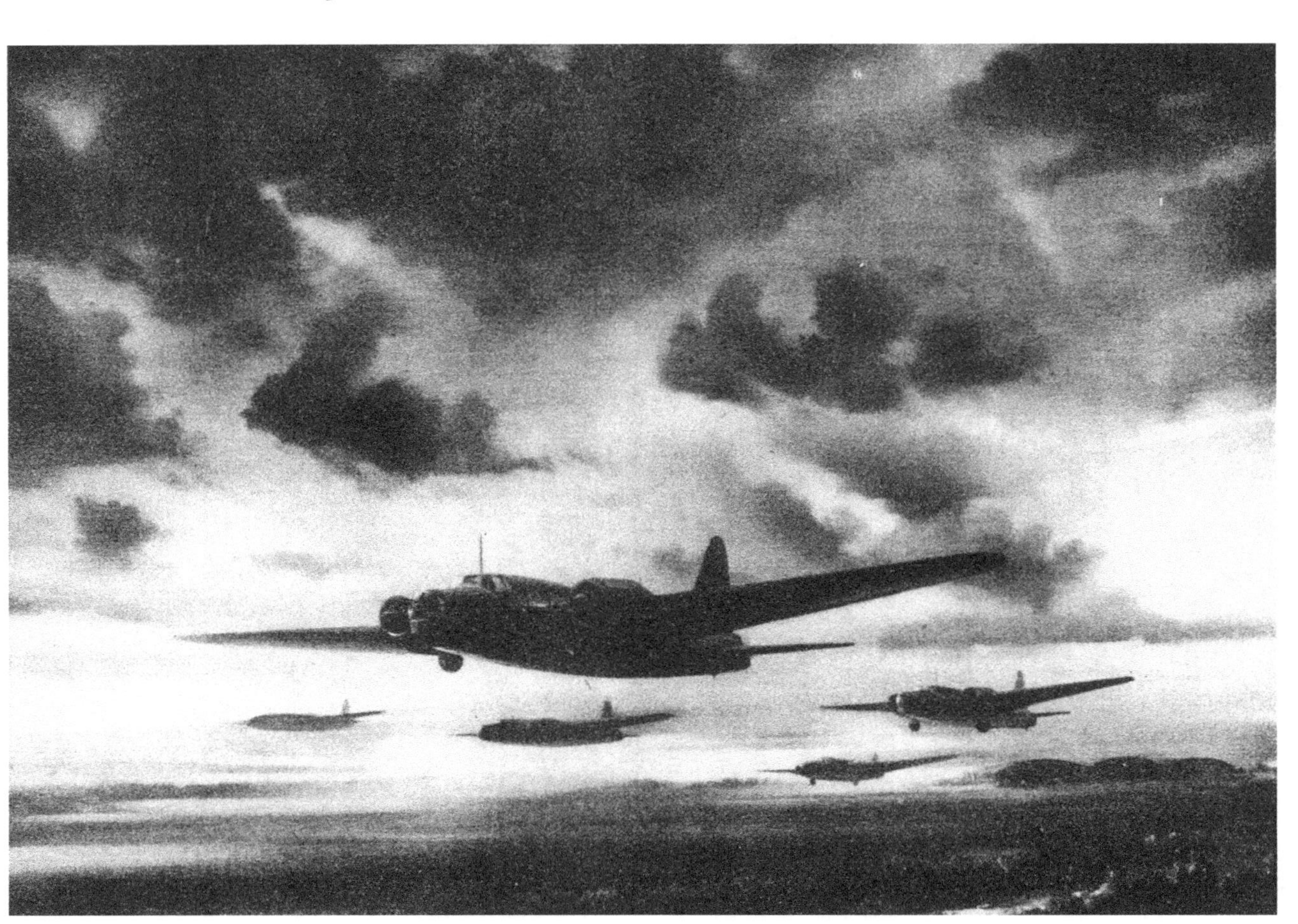

# COMPOSITION

Here is a combination of the two forms of composition that I have already described to you.

I will not analyse this one for you as it is a very straightforward composition and will serve as a test for what has gone before.

I would point out, however, that the formation of the 'planes has no important bearing in this particular drawing. Any close grouping would serve just as well as this one.

An effect of speed is not looked for in an elevation of a number of 'planes flying in formation. When flying in formation at a fair height a pilot does not get any sense of speed from watching the other 'planes in his formation. Rather it seems as though the clouds are moving past and the 'planes are stationary. The only sense of movement is that indicated by the airspeed indicator, the sound of the wind rushing past, and a slight movement of the wing tips to correct and keep the 'planes in formation.

Airspeed Oxfords

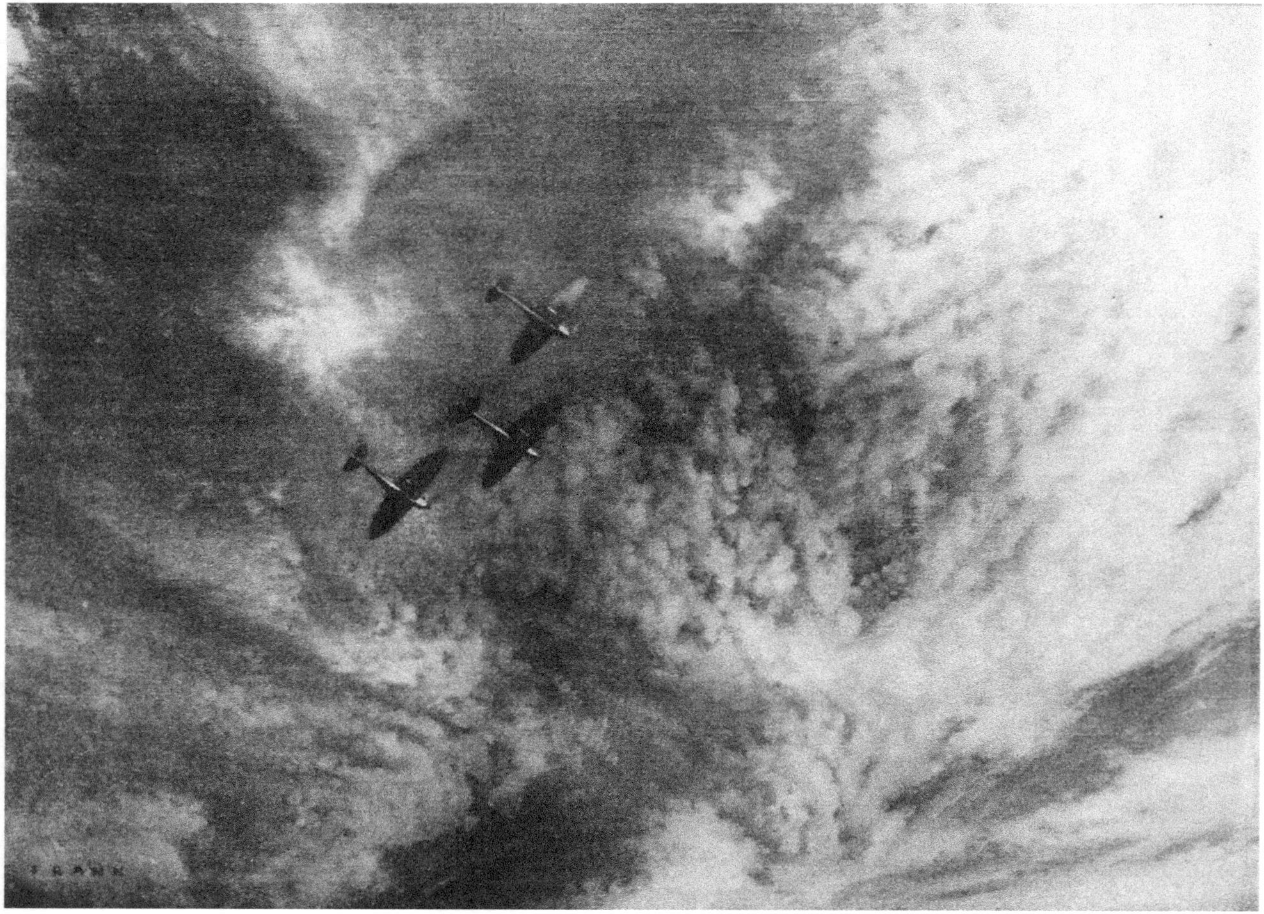

Spitfires against Alto Cirrus

All of the compositions that have gone before have relied entirely upon different cloud formations. This one especially depends on the clouds, so much so that the 'planes are only secondary in importance.

The compositional value of the clouds in this picture is best explained by a simple key drawing indicating the directional lines as this composition is rather more complicated than the others.

A study of clouds and their formations would be very useful to you, not only for pictures of aircraft but for all other drawings in which there is a sky, landscape for instance, so I would recommend that you make as many drawings of cloud studies as possible. Make notes of the time of day that the studies were made as these give a lead to the lighting, strength of tones and colour.

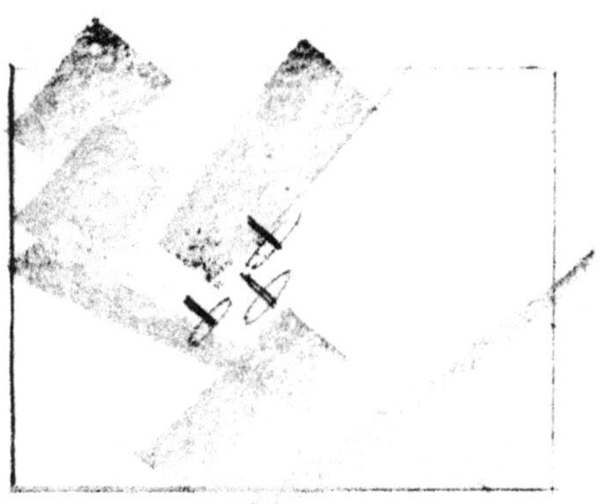

# L Y S A N D E R S

This painting was chosen to show you how the 'planes themselves can affect the composition. The clouds are taking only a minor part but other elements take their place in directing the composition. The main lines are provided by the wings of the aircraft in line and the shadows of the wings cast on to the ground. Secondary to these come the fuselage and concentration of converging lines made by the legs and 'plane struts. Equally important to these lines and masses are the shapes of the spaces which they form against the sky and the ground.

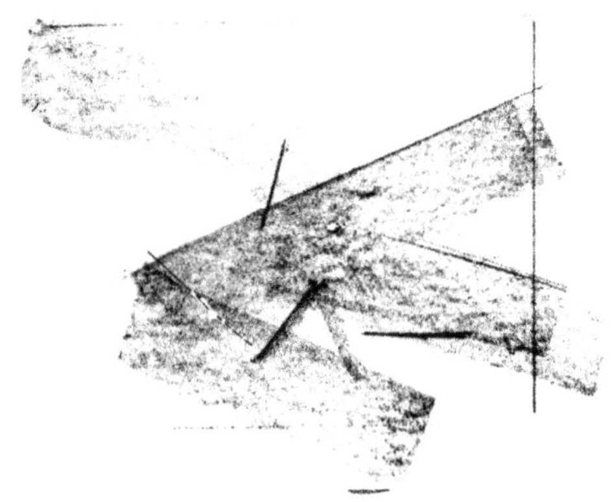

# Lysanders

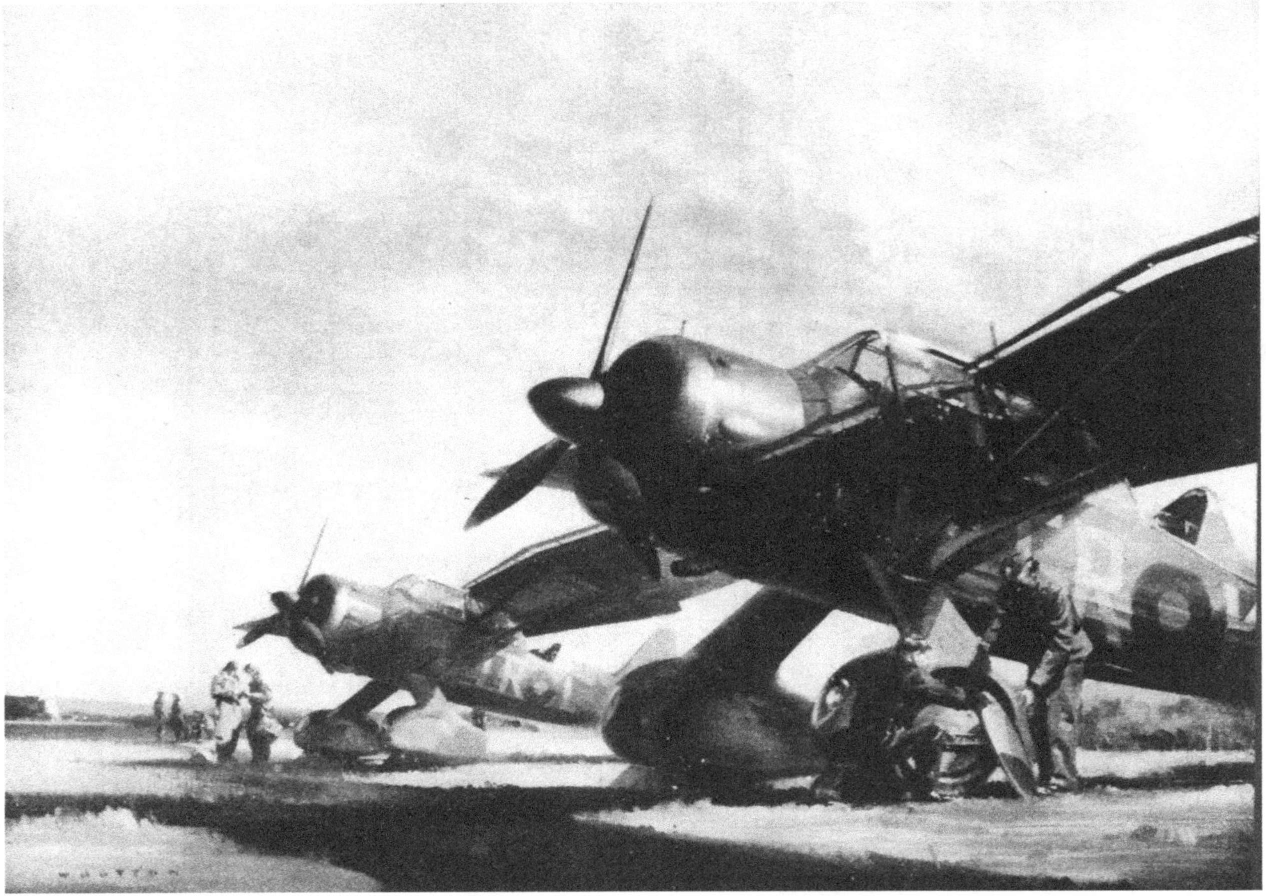

# 'BOMBING UP'

As the title suggests, this picture illustrates a typical scene at a bomber station showing Handley Page ' Hampdens ' being loaded with bombs, engines inspected and the 'planes refuelled.

The chief difficulty in a composition of this sort showing considerable activity is to prevent the composition becoming too fussy and full of separate incidents. There must be no ' details,' everything must be an essential part of the whole.

With this in view, a low horizon was chosen for the picture, the main purpose of which was to concentrate all the incidents to a similar eye level. Although this increases the difficulty of spacing the various units, it makes them easier to group and tie together. Apart from directional lines and the balance of masses, tone values were an important consideration.

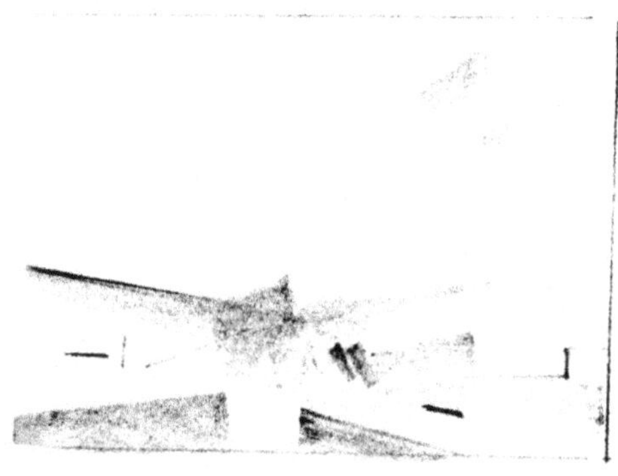

**Bombing up**

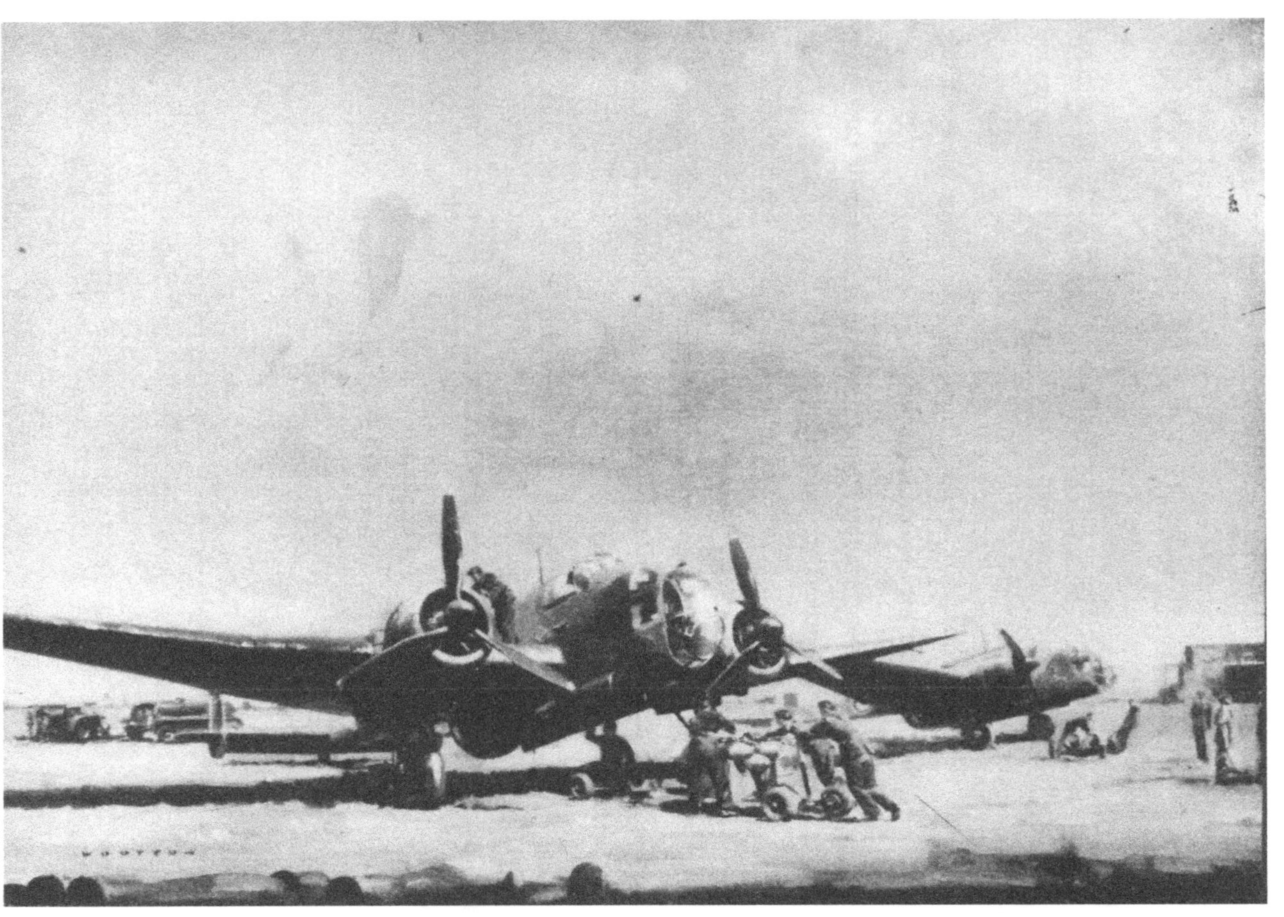

# AIRCRAFT IN ACTION

It was suggested to me that I should include in this book something about aircraft in action and how to draw them to give an impression of movement.

I am afraid that drawings of aircraft in action to be successful rely like all other pictures on composition.

These action pictures, however, are a little different in their make up, as they depend far more on directional lines and simplicity than anything else. By directional lines I don't mean speed lines. The most important thing to remember about any picture in which you are trying to illustrate something happening is that the action must be clear. Your object must be to put over the action so that it is seen and taken in instantly.

Too many incidents of equal importance in the composition will counteract all movement entirely.

A centre of vision should be decided upon, which will contain the main action. All incidentals around this point should contribute to the effect, or be left out of the picture altogether.

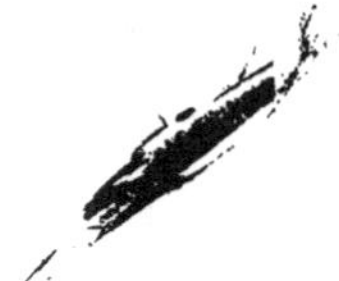

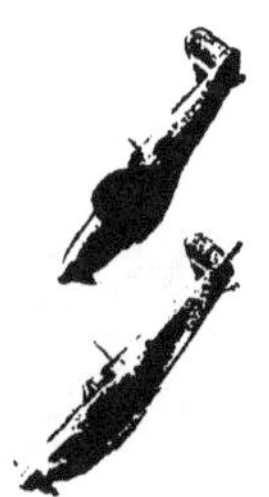

Tone values require careful thought. Although you can use your tones with more freedom in illustrations of this sort, the tones forming the background are best kept down so that they do not interfere with the 'planes.

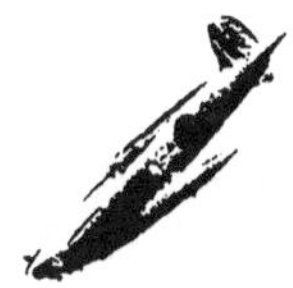

The position of the 'planes in the picture is worth consideration. They should have room to move and space to fall if you want to make the most of your composition. Try to avoid cutting the fuselage of the 'planes with the border of the picture. This may be done with compositions showing 'planes on the ground but to show a 'plane in action with only half of it coming into the picture is to destroy all sense of movement.

The directional lines in the composition made by the aircraft is another thing that deserves careful attention. The fuselage usually indicates the direction of the path the 'plane is taking. The position of the wing in relation to the movement of the 'plane will cause trouble sometimes as it sets up a strong opposition if too much is made of it.

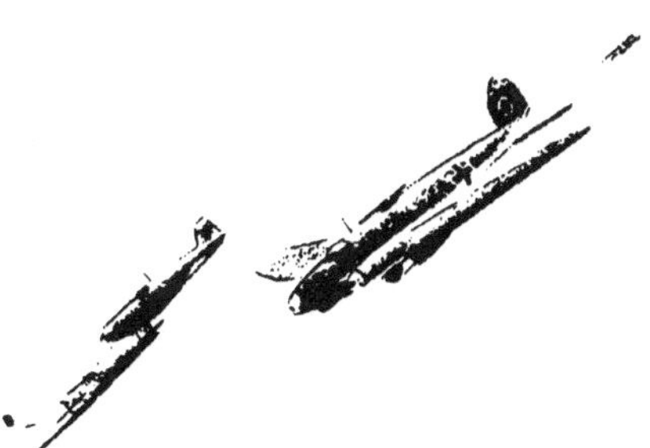

Let me illustrate what I mean about this problem with two rough sketches, taking for the incident two 'planes only, one attacking the other.

The first illustration shows a very bad arrangement although the 'planes are in quite possible positions for attack ; there is no impression of movement whatever. The angles and directional lines made by the wings and the fuselages of the 'planes are confusing. They lead your eye in all directions. The wing crosses the direction of flight on each 'plane and automatically slows the forward movement of them.

The second illustration gives a better arrangement and you will see that the wings have been foreshortened so that they do not set up awkward directional lines to distract from the diving aircraft. The attacking 'plane is converging on the pursued which helps your eye to take in the situation more quickly.

Both drawings lack a certain amount of atmosphere and excitement but that is because they have been drawn very simply to make clear the importance of the positions of the 'planes and their arrangement in the composition.

1

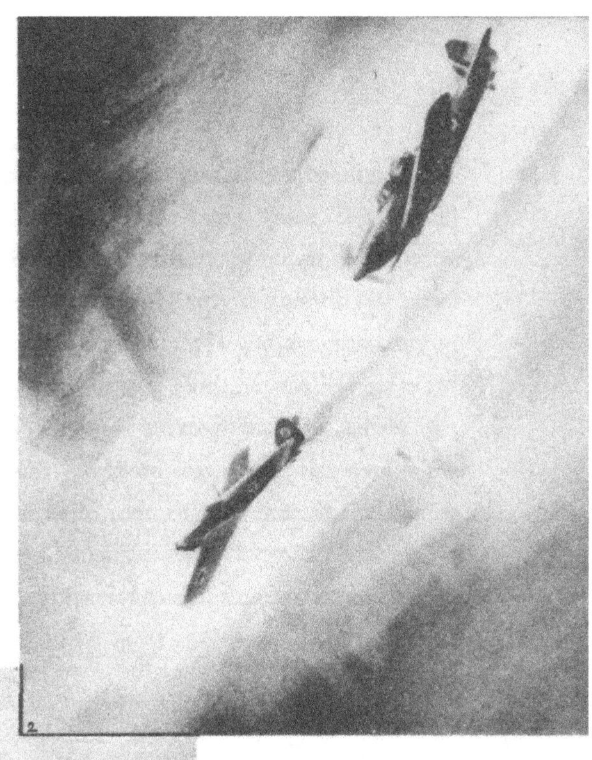

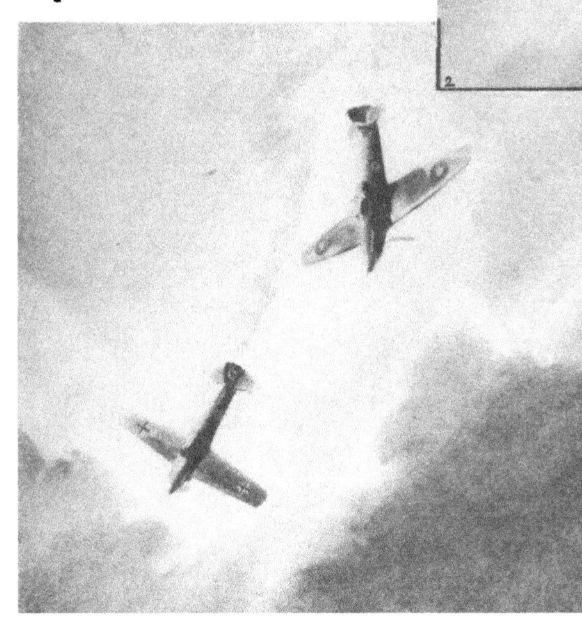

# AIR BATTLES

I mentioned a little way back that it is not wise to have in the same picture too many incidents of equal importance. This problem arises when trying to illustrate, for instance, a big air battle. If you ever try a drawing of this sort, it is a good plan to imagine yourself in the position of one of the pilots. From his point of view you would probably see two or three 'planes fairly prominently and the rest of the 'planes, whether twenty or a hundred, would be dispersed over a wide area. If they had broken formation, the individual fights would be scattered over an area of several miles.

So make the most of the incidents in the foreground and with the use of perspective and lighter tones keep the rest of the battles in the distance.

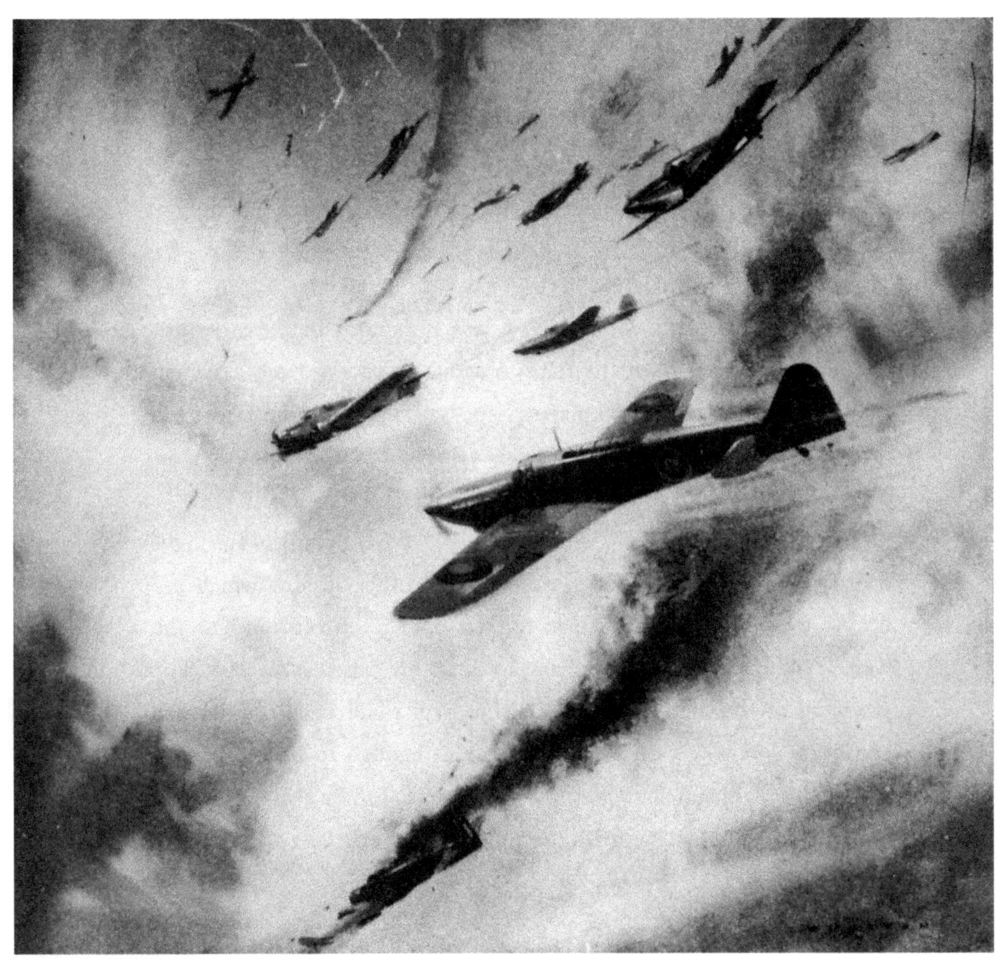

*Fulmar Fighters in action against Italians.*

# AIRCRAFT IN ACTION

Action does not always entail fighting and bombing. Reconnaissance plays a large part in the duties of the Fleet Air Arm and although it is not so spectacular as more warlike actions, reconnaissance as a subject for illustration will provide you with a lot of interesting material.

This drawing illustrates an incident in which the F.A.A. has frequently taken part. Composition was important in the structure of the picture and it will be fairly obvious to you in such a simple composition which lines and masses have been used. The wing of the 'Anson' has a definite directional value in the composition, in pointing to the raft, so has the tail 'plane.

The dark mass of the 'plane as a whole placed against the light broad mass of the sky easily balances the other masses which are not so contrasty and are rather broken up. The formation of the waves with their respective tone values are also valuable. The grouping of the men on the raft although a small detail, taking the picture as a whole, was thought important enough to have a part in the composition, and the group was arranged to form a shallow triangle or pyramid to tie up with the rescuing destroyer.



*'Anson' rescuing shipwrecked seamen.*

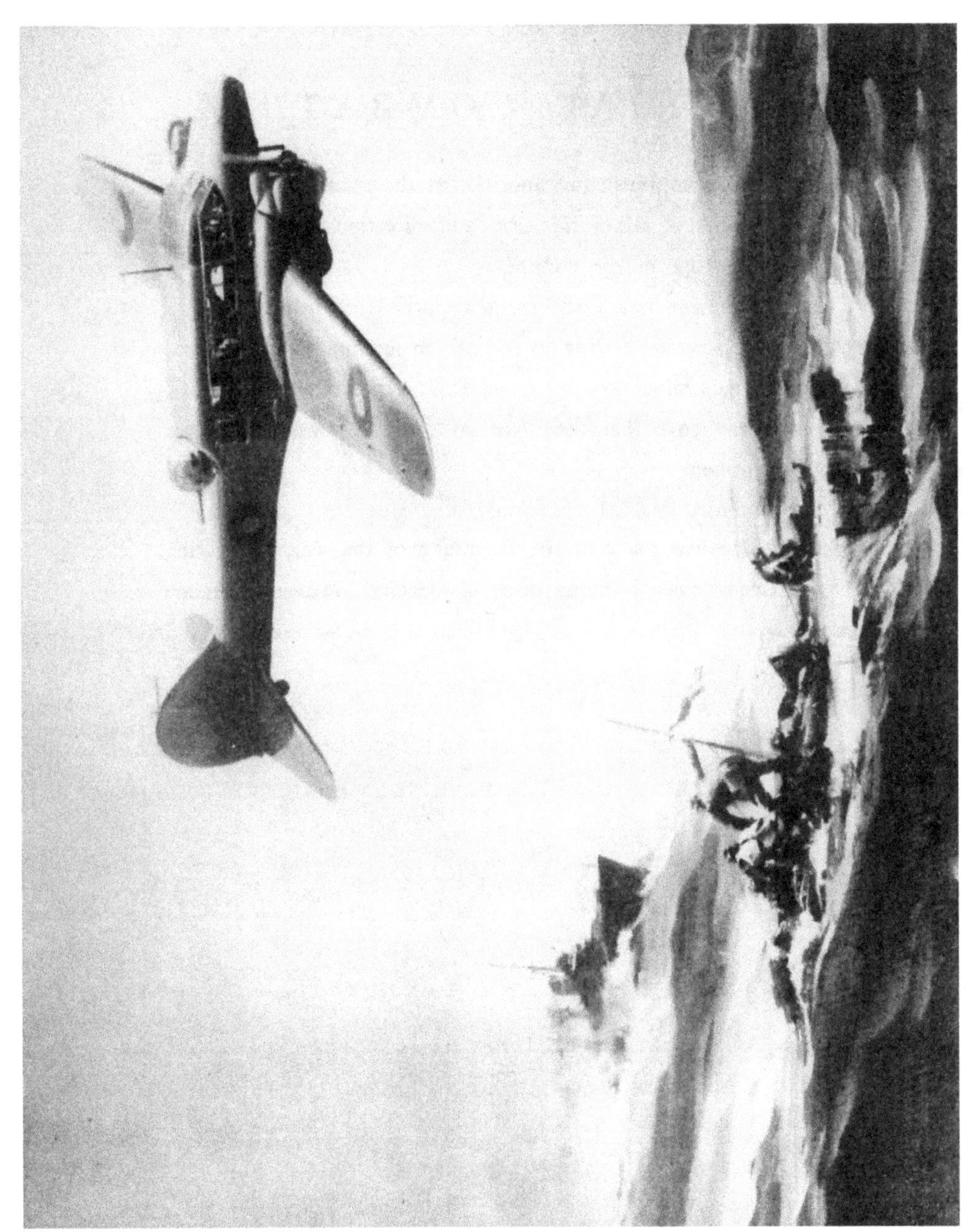

# AERIAL COMBAT

In itself this is an unusual composition as the balance of weight in masses and tones is rather topheavy and directional lines lead off the right hand edge of the picture.

This arrangement was made for the purpose of introducing an unbalanced or insecure feeling to the person looking at the picture, such as one gets when looking down from a great height. All of which goes to prove that there are no rules in composition that cannot be broken.

The drawing was made at the beginning of the war, illustrating a New Zealand pilot bringing down a Dornier 17 over a French village.



*Spitfire v. Dornier*

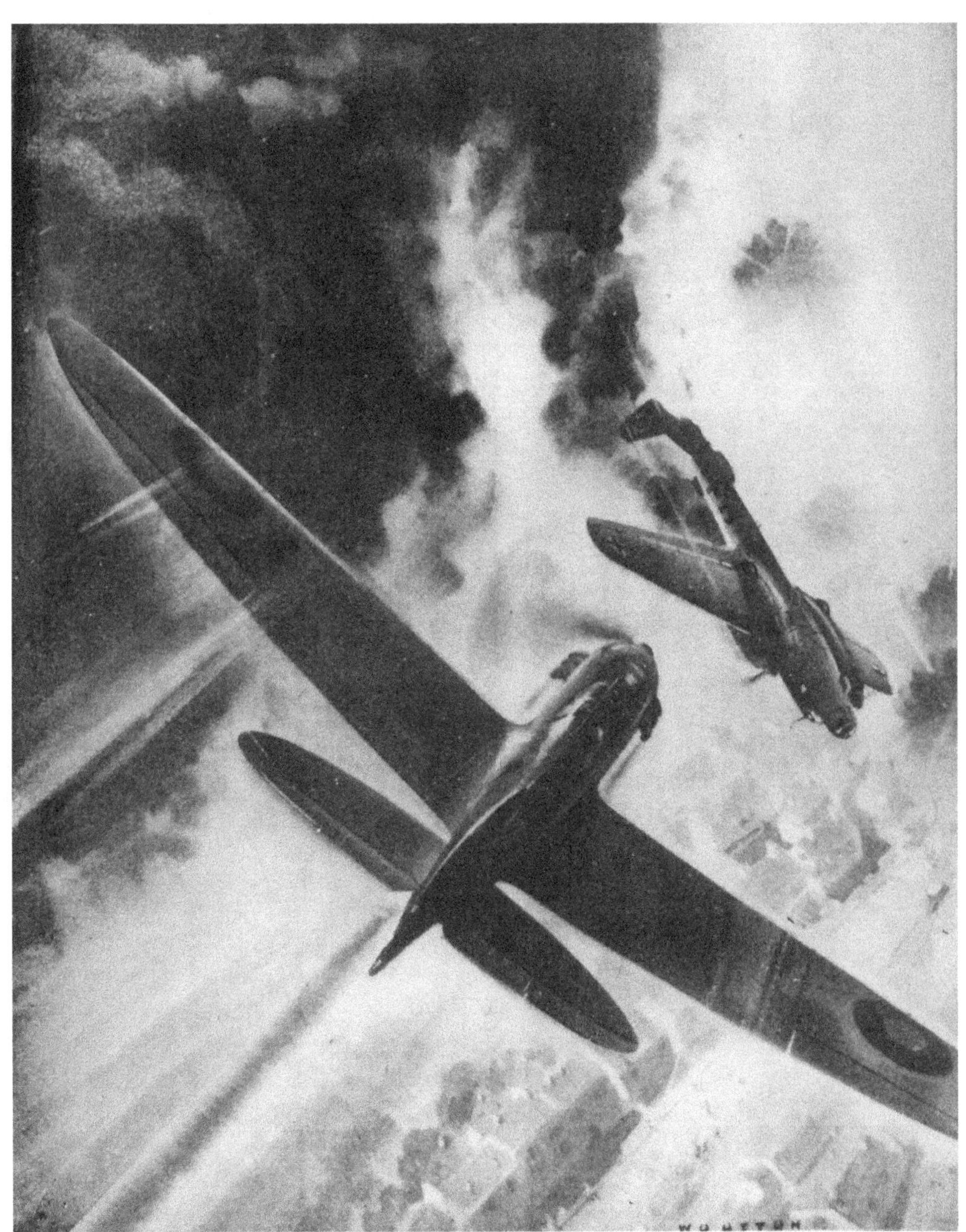

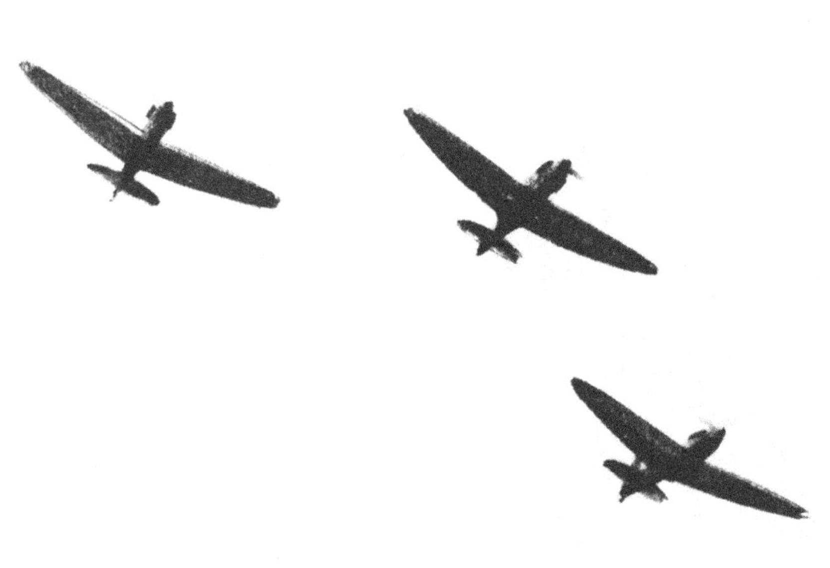

# Coachwhip Publications

## CoachwhipBooks.com

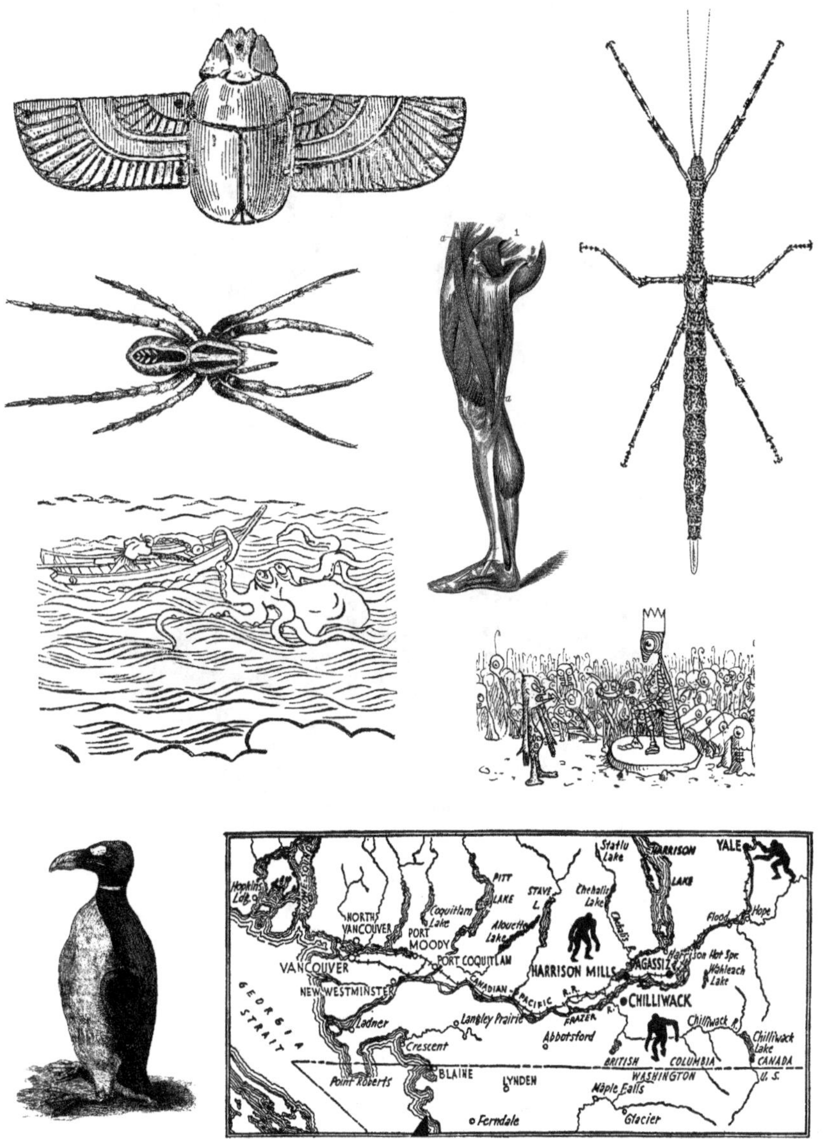

Coachwhip Publications
CoachwhipBooks.com

# TANKS

## and How to Draw Them

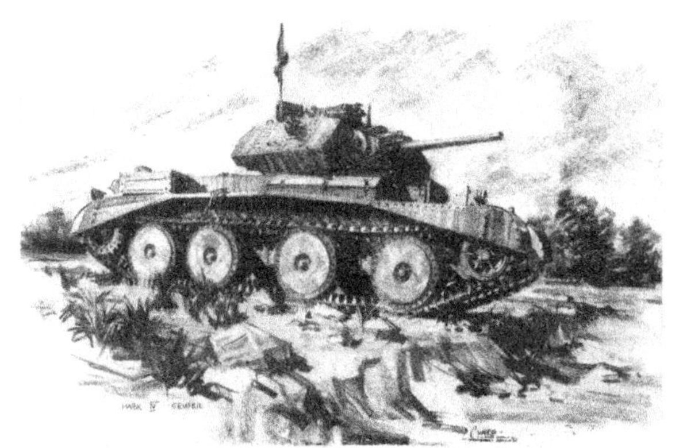

Terence T. Cuneo

ISBN 978-1-61646-021-1

# Coachwhip Publications

## CoachwhipBooks.com

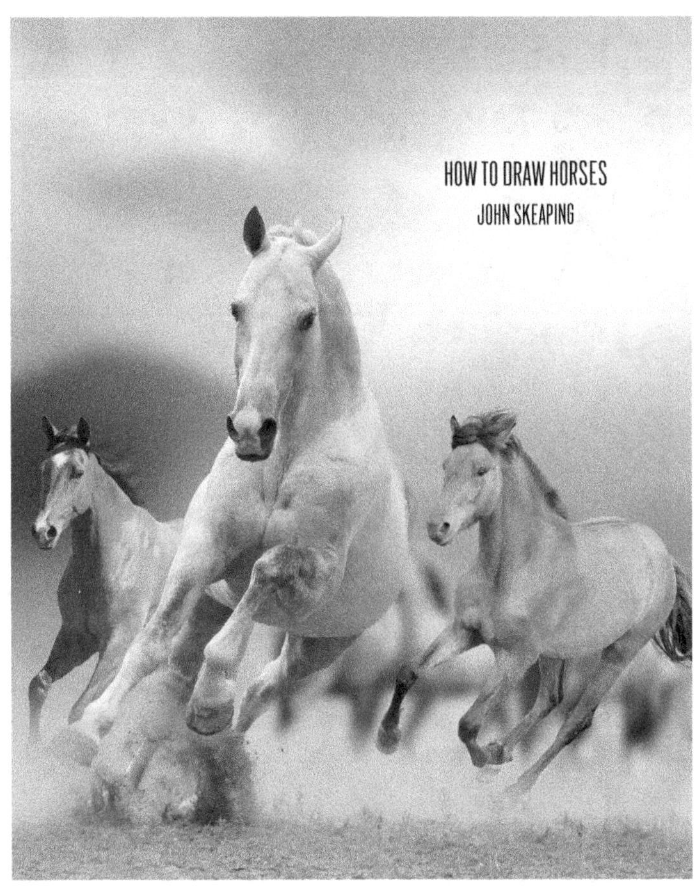


ISBN 978-1-61646-190-X

Coachwhip Publications
CoachwhipBooks.com

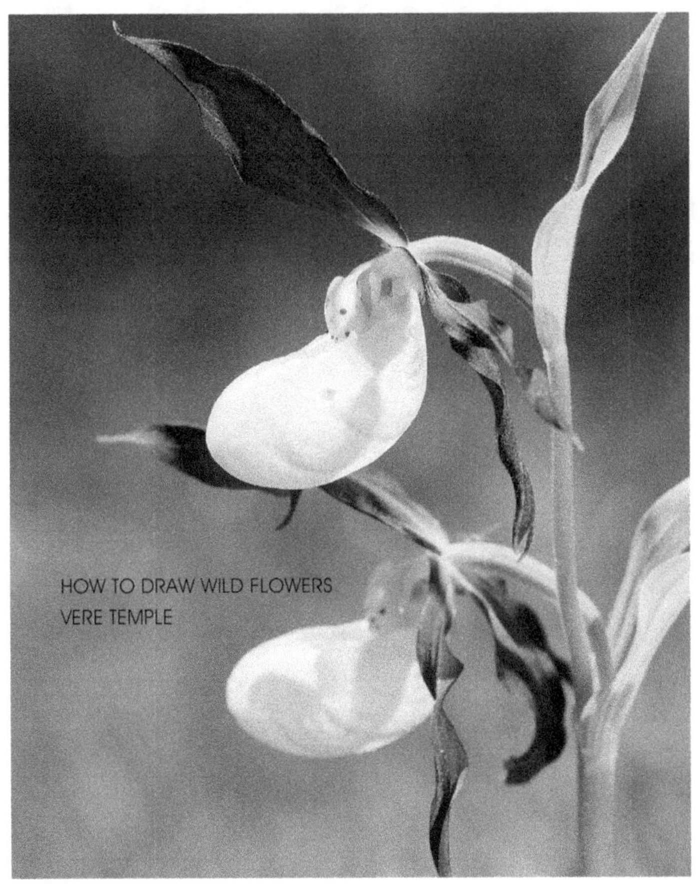


ISBN 978-1-61646-196-6

www.ingramcontent.com/pod-product-compliance
Lightning Source LLC
LaVergne TN
LVHW081301100826
845148LV00005B/941

*9781616462062*